Stretching Lessons

THE DARING THAT STARTS
FROM WITHIN

SUE BENDER

Illustrations by
Sue and Richard Bender

HarperSanFrancisco
A Division of HarperCollins*Publishers*

HarperCollins books may be purchased for educational, business, or sales pro-
motional use. For information please write: Special Markets Department,
HarperCollins Publishers Inc., 10 East 53rd Street, New York, NY 10022.

HarperCollins Web site: http://www.harpercollins.com

HarperCollins® ®, and HarperSanFrancisco™ are trademarks of
HarperCollins Publishers Inc.

FIRST HARPERCOLLINS PAPERBACK EDITION PUBLISHED IN 2002

Library of Congress Cataloging-in-Publication Data
Bender, Sue.
  Stretching lessons : the daring that starts from within / Sue Bender.—1st ed.
    p. cm.
    1. Conduct of life—Miscellanea. I. Title.

BJ1581.2.B4387 2001
170—dc1   00-049857

ISBN 0-06-251682-5 (cloth)
ISBN 0-06-251683-3 (pbk.)
02 03 04 05 06 ❖/RRD(H) 10 9 8 7 6 5 4 3 2 1

STRETCHING LESSONS

Also by Sue Bender

Plain and Simple
Everyday Sacred

CONTENTS

With love this book is dedicated to
Richard, Michael, and David
Mitzi McClosky
Laurie Snowden
Val Lagueux
Nancy Minges

Writing is my way to discover what my soul is trying to tell me.

PROLOGUE

I never plan to write a book.

Instead, something happens.

The inspiration for *Stretching Lessons* came from a four-year-old boy I have never met. A friend described a conversation she had with her nephew, Kyle.

"How big you're getting," she had told him.
"Oh, I'm bigger than that!" he replied.

A simple conversation.
A few words.
But the words went straight to my heart.

I felt goose bumps.

My body *knew* something important had just happened. But I am not someone who listens to her body. My heart and intuition, yes, but never my body. "Bigger than that!" my rational mind protested. "What does that mean?"

I didn't have an answer.

But I trusted the goose bumps.

Messages, important to hear, take me by surprise. They always come in a form I am not expecting. These tingling sensations from inside my body were a strong and visceral signal. There was something worth knowing, even if I didn't know what that "something" was.

What was my soul trying to tell me?
What were the goose bumps trying to tell me?

Learning to listen to my body was like entering a foreign land and having to learn a new language. This new language didn't depend on the things I have always been good at:

Struggle
Effort
Working hard all the time

Like a hermit crab that had outgrown its shell, I needed to stretch out of this exhausting way of conducting my life. But I seemed unwilling or unable to get out of the tight, constricted space I was in.

Kyle's words offered an invitation: Could I *dare* to be bigger? Could my mind and spirit grow in ways I hadn't thought possible?

Stretching Lessons is about that search.

Perhaps within each of us there is a need to stretch.

Perhaps within each of us there is a daring spirit that whispers to be heard.

My hope is that by telling my story, you will find the courage to trust your own voice—to listen to what <u>your</u> soul is trying to tell you. If you are willing to trust, to have faith in the unfolding, we can go on this journey together.

Together we can stretch—and dare to be as big as we really are.

All the arts we practice are apprenticeship. The big art is our life.

M. C. RICHARDS

BEGINNING

Spending too much time hunched over the computer, trying to write, I decided to sign up for a stretching class. "Just Stretch" it was called. It would be healthy, I thought, and I was prepared to be a good and earnest student and work hard, as I usually do. Instead, I heard a miraculously flexible instructor, Nancy, say:

"PRACTICE ENJOYING. DON'T PRACTICE STRUGGLING."

The suggestion was startling, revolutionary, and sweet: "Pain doesn't have to be your teacher."

"Unlearn the habit of trying," she said after we began to stretch. "It's not about trying—it's about allowing."

But *trying* is my middle name, I wanted to shout. How do I learn allowing?

Back at my desk after class, I wrote Nancy's words in large bold letters with lots of * * * * * next to each one. Though there was nothing to show on the outside, even the possibility of doing what she suggested made me feel calm inside. All I could think was, "I hope this class never ends!"

I felt like a person who'd been too long in the desert, hungry and thirsty, suddenly offered delicious, unfamiliar nectar. Nancy's last instruction rings in my ears:

"Listen to the whispers."

Could I quiet down my own noise to hear the soft whispers from within? What happened next was a shriek, not a whisper.

"Talent is doing what comes naturally," a friend announced.

"What do you think comes naturally to you?" she asked me. The answer came quickly and with great certainty:

"**STRUGGLE!** I'm an expert at STRUGGLING."

The swiftness and clarity of my response made me laugh. But it wasn't funny. My old, familiar voice of judgment chimed in: "Haven't you learned anything? Aren't you wiser?"

I <u>am</u> wiser.
And I am <u>still</u> struggling.

Have good things grown out of my exhausting habit of struggling? Absolutely. I've written two books using struggle as my method. But after seventeen years of this single-minded obsession with writing, I still didn't think of myself as a writer.

Working this way only confirmed an old belief of mine: good things will come to me, but I will have to work hard and work <u>all</u> the time to make them happen. I wondered if I also believed I had to struggle in order to earn the right be happy.

There's a difference between hard work and unnecessary suffering.

If I were composing an ad for a relationship magazine and deciding to really tell the truth about myself, I would say:

Expert at *struggle*, longing for ease. Signed: EAGER.

I'm sixty-six years old and I want to learn about ease. Even writing the word *ease* or saying it out loud has a magical effect on me. The expression on my face softens, my shoulders drop two inches, and I'm able to take a full and deep breath.

"I want to learn about ease," I announced to my wise friend Mitzi, with a determined ring in my voice. "I'm going to use my natural talent for struggle to learn how not to struggle." Sometimes, too earnest in my search for answers, I forget to laugh at myself: My *struggle toward ease.*

Mitzi told me about a time, many years ago, when she was taking a dance class in college. The teacher asked the students to imagine themselves holding a heavy ball and then lifting it over their heads. Mitzi was very busy trying to lift the heavy ball, never succeeding at getting it more than three inches above the ground, only stopping her labors for a moment when she heard the group laughing.

She looked up and saw all the students with their balls over their heads, watching her tugging at her invisible ball. She had succeeded at creating the heaviest ball.

"I don't think you always have to suffer in order to do good work," Mitzi said. "After all, I was the one who made my ball too heavy. The task hadn't been difficult. I created my own struggle."

She turned to me and asked: "Could you begin to imagine a release from the struggle? A gentler way to change?" Could I find a release that feels good and doesn't require so much hard work?

Looking at *release* on the page, I see *ease* tucked in.

Today, Valentine's Day, a card arrived with a handmade heart and, in a friend's beautiful handwriting, a reminder from Rilke:

Be patient
toward all that is unsolved in your heart.

Something happens. Nothing extreme or dramatic. A chance meeting. Something we could not have predicted, a shift, ever so slight—and our life takes a turn.

Jungian analyst Robert Johnson calls these seemingly random occurrences *slender threads*. They appear in many forms, and lead us forward—allowing our lives to unfold.

"The life of your destiny," a friend once told me.

What a splendid thought—the life of our destiny—and the image of slender threads guiding us.

The night before I was to give a talk in Salt Lake City, I attended a small dinner party to celebrate the event. Pamela, a woman in her fifties, turned to me, her voice quiet and reserved, as we were talking about talent and artists.

"I'm not an artist," Pamela said. "I have no talent."

Her words, spoken in a matter-of-fact way, made an imprint on my soul.

Again, I felt goose bumps.

I wanted to cry.

There was a long pause in the conversation. No one knew what to say. After a while, one guest after another spoke up, each relating the good deeds Pamela had done.

"Pamela carries food and clothing for the homeless in the trunk of her car," one guest began. "And food for the dogs of her homeless friends," added another.

"Pamela believes dogs love unconditionally," still another chimed in. "She knows dogs don't judge people, and for many homeless that is the only love they get." In a quiet, steady, unrehearsed rhythm, each person added a new piece of the story.

I heard myself blurt out, "Pamela, you <u>are</u> an artist!"

Pamela paused. And then, with a great deal of feeling, said, "No one has ever called me an artist!"

I looked at Pamela; her face was shining. In that moment, I saw a deeper-rooted truth, *beyond* my usual knowing:

Each of us has our own way of expressing ourselves.
Each of us has something special to give.

And it is important to value our own way of expressing ourselves—*whatever* it is.

Like Pamela, many of us do not believe there is anything special about ourselves.

I had seen something in Pamela she had not seen in herself—a bigger vision of who she was. Each of us at that table experienced Pamela's pleasure at that recognition—and her pleasure was contagious. Perhaps we had gotten a glimpse of a more inclusive sense of what art is: *the art of our lives.*

Perhaps we had also seen ourselves—who <u>we</u> are—our own worth.

I smiled, describing my *goose bumps theory of intuition* to Rachel Naomi Remen, a rare teacher, writer, healer, and friend. "Do you know anything about goose bumps?" I asked.

"Yes," she answered.

"Goose bumps happen when your soul comes close to you, breathes lightly on the back of your neck, and wakes you up."

Not trusting what we know is a terrible feeling.

I spent the last four years writing enough prologues to fill another whole book. What I was learning wasn't only about the body. Independent of my control, rich, diverse images began inhabiting my thoughts: eagle vision, red socks, flapping wings, hermit crabs, a white scarf with holes in it to allow spirit to come through—and our souls growing wings.

I kept looking for the one that stood out and shouted "Pick me!"

I kept trying to squeeze the journey into one linear and logical path labeled: straight ahead. But mine was a zigzag path. It didn't want to be contained. Finally, I remembered:

SPIRIT WORK IS MESSY!

I had known that.
But I didn't trust what I knew.

I had held back and doubted my own experience. I had limited my vision, thinking there was a *right way* to write a book, and that meant having only one image guide me. When I stopped fighting myself, I saw that all of these images reached out, grabbed at my heart and kept tugging, until I finally had to listen. All are moving me forward—helping to translate the message I felt in my heart onto the printed page.

An inherent order deeper than linear time took over.

DARING THAT STARTS FROM WITHIN

A sheltered life can be a daring life as well. For all serious daring starts from within.   EUDORA WELTY

It took me a while to appreciate how much courage the daring really takes.

I wanted, like Kyle, to be *bigger than,* but the first things I uncovered were some of the limits I had imposed on myself. When I was young, I responded to challenges the best I could, but I remembered times I ended up shrinking from being my full self.

THE AWARD

My brother and I went to camp free because our mother was the head swimming counselor. I loved camp, but felt pressured by my mother's presence. When I was eleven my counselor went to her in tears. "Sophia," she cried, "I can't manage your daughter. She's driving me crazy and she gets all the girls in the bunk to follow her."

The next year I decided to be on my best behavior.

This was a conscious choice. If I were good enough, I might possibly win the award for the Best Character in my age group at the grand awards banquet at the end of the summer. I noticed I enjoyed this new behavior as much as I had enjoyed being a frisky rule breaker.

I told no one of my hope.

Having a special secret made me happy. I felt alive admitting to myself that I wanted something—and wanted it badly. I even imagined going up to accept the award and everyone clapping. But there was a polio scare that summer and the camp had to close down early.

Instead, the awards banquet was to be held in December, at a hotel in the city. I spent the next four months thinking of nothing else but the award, waiting, hating to wait, growing more and more nervous and excited.

The night of the banquet all the campers gathered in the large ballroom, my heart beating so loud I thought I might faint. When the time finally came to announce the Best Character award for my age group, the director simply said, "There will be no award in this category this year."

What is the sound of a twelve-year-old's dream being shattered?

I hadn't told anyone beforehand, and I was too ashamed to tell anyone now. I wanted to be comforted, but I was caught in my secret. Unconsciously, I made a promise to myself: I would never, never let myself want anything so badly again.

A trap door snapped shut.

Without realizing what I was doing, I began closing down that part of myself that had dreams—not allowing my body and spirit to feel my longing. I began holding myself back from being my full self, and I was holding that in my body.

What do you want?
What does it cost?
Is it worth the price?

Yvonne Rand, a wonderful Buddhist teacher and friend, had asked me those questions. My twelve-year-old self had decided not to pay the price for wanting anything so much. Refusing to risk, I grew *smaller than.*

It took me years to learn that *not risking* was too high a price.

I attended a small public elementary school in New York City where, as an earnest student, I did my homework diligently, made good grades, and was in the "smart" class. Toward the end of sixth grade, we took a placement exam before entering the large junior high nearby.

A few days later, I happened to glance down at the teacher's desk and saw a list of names—the students destined for the *"rapid advance"* class in seventh grade.

My name was not on the list.

Perhaps in that nervous, furtive glance I hadn't seen correctly, but I was devastated. I had assumed we would all be together, and I wanted desperately to stay with my group.

Although I had always been healthy, shortly after that I started to feel unwell. My mother took me to our family doctor, then to a series of experts, who each tried to puzzle out what was wrong with me.

No one asked me what was wrong.

No one asked me if something was going on in my life at that particular moment. Had they asked, would I have been able to say? Could I have made the connection between my great disappointment and what was happening in my body?

Finally, the experts agreed.

I had developed a rapid pulse and heartbeat. It wouldn't be wise, they said, for me to go to that large school with its many stairs. My mother looked for a smaller school that didn't have steps and the only one that qualified had no rapid advance class.

That summer I wasn't allowed to go to camp. I had to stay home and rest. In the fall, I went to the smaller, gentler school.

At thirteen, I wasn't an expert on the stress theory of health.

I never understood if it was my body's resourcefulness that created the speedy pulse and racing heartbeat. But somewhere, lurking inside, I suspected I had devised a way to avoid the shame of not being in that special class.

I hid my shame. But my body knew.

When we were first married and living in Switzerland, my husband, Richard, and I would take long walks. "Are you tired? Do you need to stop for a while?" he would ask, wanting to be helpful.

"*No*" I would answer, quite definite.

Five minutes later, I couldn't move.

Geared to the exhausted push, I had only an *off*-and-*on* switch. I didn't recognize the clues that were telling me when I was at the edge of exhaustion.

How was I now going to listen to my body's whispers when I ignored its larger sounds?

My first thought was—find an image that describes how I see myself as a *body*. I marched into the studio, grabbed a batch of Crayola crayons and a big sheet of newsprint paper, sat at the table, closed my eyes, took a few deep breaths, and waited.

No image came.

I waited some more, starting to feel foolish just sitting. After a while, to keep myself entertained, I tried a technique I had learned in a class on guided imagery. I closed my eyes again and followed my breath for a few minutes. Then I pictured myself in a tranquil scene, a meadow filled with white daisies.

To my surprise, what I saw and then drew in a childlike way was a well-functioning chrome machine. Sleek, stylized, and gilded like an Oscar on the Academy Awards—or one of those silvery robots in the Woody Allen movie *Sleeper*.

In no way did I resemble it, even symbolically. What did fit was that I had taken my body for granted. I treated it like a machine, but not one of those beloved possessions, a car, for example, whose doting owner takes it regularly for oil changes, tune-ups, checkups, and other preventive maintenance. I just kept pushing Chrome—wondering how was I ever going to do all the things I wanted to do. I didn't even take pleasure in the fact that my body was working well.

When the machine didn't break down, I ignored it.

While living in Zurich, I went to the Swiss equivalent of Goodwill and came home with the top half of an authentic suit of medieval armor. I have no recall what possessed me to buy it, but the armor has sat on our living room floor wherever we have lived ever since. Now when I walk past this chromelike object I ask:

How do I—we—begin taking off our armor?

VISION

I told a friend how hard it was to begin taking off my armor. I felt exposed and fragile realizing how much of myself I had shut down for so many years. Her words are now in my heart. I remind myself, almost daily, of what she said.

"Sue, there's so much to support you.
"Maybe you don't know that yet!"

I began a *practice:* Allow myself to feel supported.

VIDEO

Sometimes the image we give to the world is different from what we feel inside.

A number of years ago, I got very depressed.

I wasn't sure why I was so sad, but nothing I did made the feeling go away. Finally, a good friend, a psychiatrist, suggested I come to his office. He set up his video camera, and said, "Talk to the TV screen as if you were talking to a therapist or to an understanding, wise friend." He assured me that whatever I said would be private.

When he played the tape back for me, I saw on the screen a pleasant-looking middle-aged woman describing in a rather pleasant way how terrible she was feeling inside. The words rang true. No editing or censoring. But for only two out of the twenty minutes did the expression on my face and the look in my eyes actually convey my unhappiness.

I listened and looked, stunned.

The great discrepancy between my appearance and the pain I felt shocked me. I finally understood how Richard, who was sympathetic, continued to see me as a functioning person.

During those six months of feeling miserable, whatever strength and resources I could muster were needed to do my work, cook meals for my husband and sons, and hold myself together. I didn't have the strength to go to dinner parties or to have people over for dinner.

After six months the dark mood lifted as mysteriously as it had appeared.

But once I was feeling better, I still didn't want to be part of these social events. I did feel a deep need to quiet down enough to hear what my body and spirit were trying to tell me.

Pulling back into myself, I wondered if unconsciously my desire had been to change the status quo—make a shift in my life—but I didn't have the courage or trust myself or Richard enough to say, "I don't want to go to dinner parties anymore. I don't want to have people over for dinner. For my well-being, I need to retreat."

Could depression sometimes be a necessary step toward change?

Could my *smaller than* be an invitation to stretch?

I no longer went to parties or gave them; instead, I became a relative recluse.

At some point I began to think of myself as a hermit crab. A hermit crab leaves its shell to move out in the world and returns when it's ready. I went out into the world, gave talks, and then, after a while, sometimes, a very little while, began to feel the pull, the need to come back home.

I call it reclusive, but it's really not. With the phone and fax machines humming and the dishwasher breaking down, I'm very much connected to the world outside. But the deeper need to stop, listen to the wisdom of my body, and go back into my shell remains. This movement is the opposite of putting on armor; it is moving deeper within.

To settle oneself on oneself.   KATAGIRI ROSHI

I adored my father.

"Be with me," he demanded when I was a child, but never saying the words out loud. "I love you," his unspoken message continued, "and I need you to be around <u>all</u> the time—to make me feel good about myself."

In moderation, that mandate might have been fine, but his need felt excessive and not negotiable. "I'm being asked to do too much," I silently cried.

Sometimes I spoke up and told him my problems and upsets. He would seem to listen, then say, "As long as you're happy," as if he hadn't heard a word.

I realized I had never felt *seen* by my father.

Years later, when I was grown, married, with children of my own, I would visit my parents in Florida. My father always wanted me to join him—at the pool, playing cards with his friends, going to the market for my mother. One particular day I decided to say aloud what I was feeling and needing.

"I'd like to go to look at the ocean," I said, longing to be alone.

"I'll go with you," was his immediate response.

"No," I said, as gently but firmly as I could, "I'd <u>really</u> like to spend an hour by myself."

"What's the matter?" he asked, with the saddest look on his face. "Don't you love me anymore?"

I loved him, and I did indeed feel loved. But his response startled me. In that moment, I saw that even when I was young, I had unconsciously devised a strategy to survive, to keep from being overwhelmed by his demands. If I kept constantly moving, involved in many, many projects, it would be hard for him, and later others, to catch me. It was my way to create a safe boundary. Now, looking back, I call what I had learned to do:

Flapping my wings.

On that day when he asked, "Don't you love me anymore?" I was still struggling not to feel constrained by his need.

I had always imagined myself as a frisky, good-spirited, independent, mildly rebellious child—I certainly hadn't thought I was squashed. But I never said, "I <u>won't</u>" aloud. If I said no, I was afraid I wouldn't be loved; if I stood still, I might be devoured. Flapping, being busy, was a strategy for cutting off feelings.

My only choice was to become a master of motion.

Sometimes things have to get worse before they start getting better.

So many people had said that yoga would be good for me, for anyone, that I finally signed up for a beginners' class. Doing what seemed like a gentle partner stretch, I felt something pull just above my ankle. I continued in the stretch.

"No pain, no gain," my negative motivator declared.

The few times I've treated myself to a massage, when the masseur asked which I preferred—Gentle? Firm? Very deep?—I would always request the deepest, the one that would hurt the most, thinking it would do the most good.

"At my age, if I paid attention to every ache and pain I'd be in real trouble," I added.

It turned out that I had hurt my Achilles tendon in the yoga class, but didn't know it right away. I did know the myth of Achilles. His mother, hoping to make her son immortal, held him by his heel and dipped him into the river Styx, the river of immortality.

The only part of Achilles' body that didn't get submerged in the water was his heel. This became his vulnerable spot. Years later, he was killed, hit by an arrow in that very place.

At the time, I refused to acknowledge my vulnerable spot. My wound wouldn't stop me! This refusal to listen to the wisdom of my body became my *Achilles' heel.*

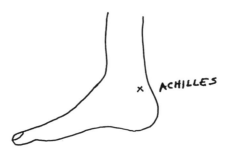

This behavior wasn't an example of being *bigger than;* rather, it was being *more stubborn than,* as I continued my early morning aerobic classes. I didn't dream of canceling a three-week book tour. Proud of my lean luggage, I stubbornly insisted on carrying it on and off the plane. My leg hurt, but when the tour was over, I went back to aerobics. Only a great deal of pain finally got me to notice—and stop.

I had no choice.

Several years later, without having tripped on anything I was aware of, I fell. I crashed down on the cement sidewalk headfirst. I had to sit there for what felt like forever at the time, and then I raised myself with great difficulty off the ground. I had a huge bump on my head and a left arm that didn't bend.

This wasn't a whisper. This was a shriek.

Did I listen? Did I finally understand my Achilles' heel?

Not yet.

The next morning I asked Richard to drive me to Café Milano and very slowly, in pain, walked up the stairs, thinking of a conversation I had with a friend years ago during a bout with a fever.

"What will it take to get you to stop?" she had asked. "A temperature of 102? 103? 105?

"Insanity is doing the same thing over and over and expecting different results."

Though I tried my best to avoid feeling the pain from the fall, the pain seemed even more determined to stay. A friend's recommendation—"He's gifted, and the work is gentle"—brought me to Ofer's class. "The work is called Feldenkreis," she added. After the first class, I asked Ofer, a slim man with an Israeli accent, what Feldenkreis means.

"The short answer is it's about learning to know yourself better in your body."

"I <u>know</u> rest is good for me," I told Ofer after class. "But if anyone tries to be helpful and suggests that I take time out to rest, the assignment only becomes one more thing on my *should-do* list. Even when I relabel it *sacred idleness,* I am still successful only at not resting."

"It's called trial and error," Ofer told me, "not trial and success."

I laughed, remembering Alexander Graham Bell's response to his assistant, who was hopelessly discouraged because of their many, many failures while trying to invent the telephone.

"We've learned a thousand ways that didn't work," answered Bell, optimistic.

Another version credits Thomas Edison, who, asked how he felt about failing so many times, replied:

"I never failed once. It was a two-thousand-step process."

SOFTLY

"What if you have an old habit that gets in your way?"

I asked Ofer this question one day. "You don't have to spend your time trying to change old habits," he said with conviction. *"Build better ones."*

As I daydreamed about building better habits, the word *softly* bubbled up from someplace inside. I mentioned *softly* to Ofer.

"Looking for a way to be softer really pays off," he said. "Those who move most gently will notice the most difference. The aim is not for the greatest movement—but the smoothest one.

Treat yourself gently.

As he said these words, I heard the sound of one of those huge bronze bells I once heard in an ancient Zen temple in Japan. The sound of the bell continued to vibrate in my ear, and I felt goose bumps—a reminder of what is possible if we don't work so hard.

INVISIBLE

Not being seen can be a terrible feeling.

When we moved from New York to California thirty years ago, I had a neighbor who was also from the East. Our husbands taught at the University of California, and our sons played together. When we saw each other on the street, we'd stop for a moment and say hello.

Four years after our first meeting, we happened to meet and were having our "by chance" hello. During our conversation, apropos of something she said, I mentioned that I had gone to Harvard for a master's degree.

"<u>Why didn't you tell me?</u>" she asked, her eyes opened wide and a startled expression on her face. "I didn't know you were intelligent!"

Some people will <u>never</u> see us—that doesn't mean we're not there.

My ritual on airplanes is to read magazines, and I'm always eager to get on the plane early, to get the best selection. I was headed to Sun Valley, Idaho, to give a talk at the Sun Valley Library, when I read an article describing a woman's trek with the aborigines. On the fourth day the aborigines stopped.

"Why are you stopping?" she asked, surprised and puzzled. "There is nothing here."

At first, the aborigines didn't seem to understand the question. Finally, after a long silence, one of the elders spoke:

"We're waiting for our souls to catch up!"

Sitting on the plane, I felt goose bumps—a moment of recognition.

At the Sun Valley Library, I read "Little Sabbaths" from *Everyday Sacred*. It's about the importance of taking time, even a few minutes, to stop in the midst of a too-busy day. The image of the aborigines pausing came into my heart.

Now, when I am wise enough to stop and savor a little sabbath, I take a few extra deep and quiet breaths and remember:

I'm waiting for my soul to catch up.

Every blade of grass has its Angel that bends over it and whispers,
"Grow, grow." TALMUD

When I first met Pamela and heard her say, "I'm not an artist," the goose bumps I felt signaled a deep insight beyond my rational thinking. What I saw was a *spirit stretch,* for it wasn't only about Pamela—it was the intrinsic worth in each of us.

When my friends and I talk about times we feel invisible, constricted, or full of doubt, I think of Nelson Mandela's beautiful words:

The world will not fall apart if we let ourselves express our vastness. It is more likely the world will stop falling apart when we do.

How important it is to value our own way of expressing ourselves—whatever it is.

Valuing our way is how we whisper, *"Grow, Grow."*

OPENING

I was delighted when one day in stretching class Nancy asked us to stand on all fours and imagine ourselves as hermit crabs. This wasn't hard, since I had already experienced myself as one, though I hadn't perfected it yet. We were to bend back slowly, very slowly, moving one vertebra at a time.

Nancy instructs us to move softly, lightly, but I feel the weight of my shell, a very heavy shell. This heavy protective shell is weighing me down, and I cannot enjoy this movement with ease.

Suddenly, I feel my shell has become too small.

Just then, Nancy says, "Can you imagine your shell getting bigger? Can you have more space inside?" Imaging myself as a hermit crab isn't hard. Why is it so much harder to make my internal space as large as I wish?

Why do I cramp within my shell when I could choose to be more spacious?

Recently I learned that a hermit crab doesn't have its own shell. The crab's work is to find an abandoned shell and make that its home. When the crab starts to grow too big for that shell, it searches around and finds another one to suit its new size. The crab is particular, going back and forth from shell to shell, trying them on, like pairs of shoes, until it finds the right fit.

What do we do when we start to outgrow our shells?

What choices do we make, and how do we make them, as we become *bigger than* we were?

"I choose them all."

I love that bold statement. Kathleen Norris was quoting four-year-old Thérèse of Lisieux, who was asked to choose one ribbon out of a batch presented to her. I love it because it reflects so clearly the heart of my dilemma. Thérèse grew up to be a saint.

I felt anything but saintlike loading my car for a ten-day work retreat: two milk crates crammed with files; fifteen folders—red, white, black, and gray—bursting with scraps of paper, the first seedlings for stories; too many books to read even with the luxury of ten days away; and many stuffed files labeled: SORT. Why do I feel the need to take almost every scrap of paper?

It's easier to know what I don't want.

It's so much harder to know what I do want.

How do I choose? How does anyone choose? How do we sort out our priorities when we want to choose them all?

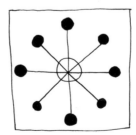

CLARITY

"**I choose them all,**" I told a friend.

"It's okay to have lots of options, as long as you know what you want," she said.

She went on to describe making a plan with her eight-year-old neighbor to go to the zoo. "Shall we go across the bridge? Should we take a bus?" she asked.

"We can go however you want, but we have to get there!"

NEW YEAR'S CLASS

I'm one of those people who never manage to stay up until midnight on New Year's Eve. However, I do love making a long list of resolutions. To celebrate the New Year, Nancy taught a special class.

"Today's class will be a *letting go* process," she began. "Is there something you'd like to get rid of?"

Without a moment's hesitation, I had my answer. I wanted to let go of feeling I had to struggle all the time. "NO! NO!" a voice screamed inside me. "I WON'T!"

Stunned by the vehemence of my response, I heard Nancy say, *"Letting go can be acceptance."* We should make contact with the very thing we wanted to let go of—give it more space to be there in our lives. She added,

"We spend so much time trying to fix ourselves—rather than having ourselves.

"The more you can feel in your body—the more you can release."

Why, I wondered, would I want to accept the very thing I longed to let go of? Just as I was about to raise my hand and ask, she said,

"We only get good at what we practice.
Nothing changes if you never do anything different.

"Change comes not from more effort—it comes from an inner soft-ening." I didn't really understand what that meant, but I <u>did</u> like the sound of *softening* and the feeling in my body when I imagined an inner softening. In that moment I had a glimpse of ease.

Time went quickly after that.

As a closing ritual, she passed around a basket filled with packets of seeds and asked us to choose one. When the basket came to me, I did not choose them all. Instead, I picked Nasturtium.

I love nasturtium for its intense orange color and its ability to grow almost anywhere. Feeling tender toward this unexpected gift of *spirit seedlings,* I held the small packet of seeds in my hand, looked down, and saw written on the package:

NASTURTIUM. **Thrives under stress.**

ALIVE STRUGGLE

Shortly after Nancy's workshop and having planted the nasturtium, I happened to read the obituary of the artist Willem de Kooning: "He never knew precisely where he was headed. He dreaded resolution. He was secure in insecurity. . . .

"Everything about his art shivers with uncertainty. . . .
"He made his pictures with no fear, but a lot of trembling."

Now, I plan to invite de Kooning's **alive struggle** into my life.

These last few months, the more I declared my intention to have more ease, the stronger my "I WON'T!" voice grew. The first thing I needed to do to feel more ease was to cross off things I had been ignoring on my to-do list. But the more I tried to force a commitment to do these things, the fiercer became the refusal—a powerful saboteur.

Every time I said, "I *should*," I set the rebel in motion.

My refusal, my own tyranny over myself, was democratic, extending to phone calls, letters, e-mail, and faxes concerning my work and even from people I really cared about. Although I take pride in being responsible, I was racing full speed ahead toward open rebellion. "I WON'T" was now on automatic.

I had stated my intention to listen to the whispers of my body. Nancy, Ofer, and others made suggestions, even gave me assignments, gentle, modest, and doable. Did I do them? Of course not. I refused—although I knew and believed that doing these things would be good for me.

I remembered that, as a three-year-old, I had known what to do when, emotionally, too much was demanded of me. I just didn't do it. I had never said, "I WON'T!" to my father. I didn't say it then. And I wasn't saying it now.

"You're a rebel without a clue," a friend laughed.

Now that I had an understanding of the dynamic with my father, I could see why I was perpetually in motion—and why my "I WON'T!" voice drained so much good energy.

A heavy weight lifted.

I had another choice.

Why not make friends with "I WON'T!"? On the top of a big piece of blank white paper I wrote:

"I WON'T" LIST

All the things I had successfully resisted went on the list. With softer, kinder eyes, I read my list. Now I could appreciate my resistance. My "I WON'T!" voice, that voice I thought of as rebellious, wasn't only acting out—it was trying to take care of me when too much was coming at me all at once. I can imagine it saying:

"SLOW DOWN. Take care. Be present."

I could say yes to "I WON'T!"

With acceptance, I began inching my way out of my shell. A space opened inside me and I felt *bigger than* I had been. Before even noticing what I was doing and without a great deal of struggle, I began crossing things off the list with ease. *Should* became WANT.

A habit learned can also be unlearned.

The revenge of the itsy-bitsies, I call it, and though the words have a comical ring, feeling overwhelmed by too many tiny, little demands is not the least bit funny. When all my old remedies failed, I decided to go to the hypnotist who had helped me once before. She suggested doing something with past lives, but I wasn't the least bit interested. I wanted to know what to do <u>now,</u> right now.

That tight part of me that wants to be in control must have surrendered, because I found myself in a mild trance. I imagined I was in a past life, a leader of a group of about one hundred and fifty women. The setting was back when people were burned at the stake for disobedience—refusing to denounce their beliefs. We were threatened—besieged. To save my community from disaster, I volunteered, offered myself up—to be burned at the stake.

In my reverie, and even when I woke, this choice seemed natural. This was <u>my</u> responsibility, my way to do service. Why wasn't I afraid? Was it because I believed so deeply that only through struggle and sacrifice could I be of use to others?

I had come face-to-face with a *hidden assumption* I had been carrying around with me, buried under all the things I knew I consciously believed. In order to do good, to contribute—and earn the right to be happy—one must struggle and suffer. This belief had been guiding much of my behavior.

I knew it wasn't true.

I also knew that unconscious beliefs have even more power to affect outcomes than the ones we are aware of. I <u>did</u> want to contribute. I wanted that enormously. But I didn't want to exhaust myself and run on empty in my desire to help others. I longed to find another way—and I felt that longing in my body.

I didn't know what to do.

Rather than make a black-and-white choice, I began a practice. My intention was to listen to my inner voice. No matter what was happening on the outside, each choice, each decision, small or large, would first have to make sense on the inside.

I began designing my life from the inside out.

All I knew, and all I could trust, was to be as true to that interior voice as I could and then act from that place. Years later, I heard M. C. Richards describe it as:

Integrating one's inner search with one's outer practice.

THE BATTERY

I believe we can learn from everything.

This particular entrenched belief gives me a great deal of pleasure. One day, feeling exhausted, my sinuses letting me know I had been pushing when I was on empty, I decided to be easy on myself and pick up burritos for dinner. When I came out of the restaurant, my car wouldn't start.

Dead.

I kept trying. After half an hour the engine ignited and I was able to get the car up the hill to my house, but early the next morning the car was dead again. "A reflection of my insides," I told Richard. "Call the AAA and have it towed," he suggested. "I think it might be serious."

When my rescuer came—Lem was his name—he opened the hood, looked for a few minutes, and said,

"You're not connected to your battery. That's all."

"That's a wonderful message, Lem," I said, grinning from ear to ear. "A message from the universe telling me I have to stay connected to my battery—my own energy, my 'juice'— what I need."

I rambled on, delighted and relieved with his prognosis. "I believe we can learn from anything that happens to us."

Lem looked puzzled and said, "Lady, it's only a car!"

EFFORT

"I'm ready to throw away my crutches!" I declare to Ofer.

"Don't throw away your crutches until you learn to use your legs," he said.

"Do you really think it's possible to do things with less effort and more ease?" I asked him earnestly.

"Of course," he replied. "But working with *ease* is counter to our culture. We're trained in limitations." Even people who sense an enormous change in themselves may still ignore the change in their life so they can continue in the way of effort. They say to themselves, "This is an enormous change, but it didn't really happen because I didn't really make an effort."

I must be one of those people. Once I spent an hour struggling in a particularly challenging class he gave, unable to follow his instructions, my brain and body exhausted. Hearing him repeat "Be gentle to yourself" only annoyed me, and I was furious toward him and angry at myself for being so inept. I must be really worthy right now!

"Why doesn't he come over?" I whined to myself. "I'm trying and failing. It's not fair. He sees I don't understand the lesson. Why doesn't he show me what I should be doing?"

After class, I had a cup of tea with Ofer, a fifteen-minute ritual we've established. I told him how upset and frustrated I was during class, and how I was annoyed that he wasn't helping me out of my confusion.

"It can't be healthy to spend an hour practicing unsuccessful ways of doing the lesson," I declared. "I don't want to succeed at failing!"

"In matters of learning," Ofer said, "rushing is a waste of time.

"There's as much value in knowing how <u>not</u> to do something as how to do it."

Knowing the rhythm of our body helps us know the pace to set.

Diana is an instructor of Jin Shin Jyutsu, the practice of finding balance in the body by gently stimulating pulse points to bring them into harmony. I had gone to her because the pressure of flapping my wings all the time was wearing me out. I was exhausted.

"You're a fine racehorse," she said, taking my pulse. "You came into the world that way."

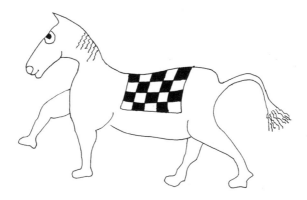

I was surprised that she could know me simply by feeling my pulse. Somewhere in my body, I knew what she was talking about. An unexpected metaphor had presented itself. Here I was, an animal with four legs whose specialty was being in motion.

"At least a racehorse knows when it's time to rest. I just keep running. I want more choices than full speed ahead and collapse," I told Diana.

"Our restlessness is because we're fighting something," she said. "We're fighting ourselves in some deep essential way.

"When we can be who we are—that's how we come to rest."

EXCEDRIN

"Each of us has our own unique motion," Nancy said, "as unique as our thumbprint."

I smiled, thinking I had the rhythm of a racehorse. "It's okay to be a racehorse, Sue, but you don't have to run every day in the Kentucky Derby," Richard added. Then I stopped daydreaming and heard Nancy say:

"Opening up will come from slowing down.

"See what comes alive from resting."

Whenever I think it will be good for me to rest, my "I WON'T" voice surfaces. I fear that if I stop, I'll never get up again.

Thirty years ago, when I lived in New York, sometimes I would get headaches. When we moved to Berkeley, life began to feel easier. The headaches stopped, but once in a while I still got a good one. Just like the TV commercial says, I'd take two Excedrin, get into bed for half an hour, and STOP. I would lie there, very still, until the headache went away. I've always given Excedrin the credit.

It never dawned on me that *stopping* had made the difference.

Nancy raised a question when I first started stretching and I have now taken that question into my body and made it my own:

If we never pause long enough to get to know the silence, how will we know what possibilities it contains?

Last week a friend gave me a fishing lesson—just what I needed. When I work, I hardly come up for air. I need more play in my life, more play in my work. The writing sometimes runs me. Even if I love what I'm doing, I get too deadly serious and one-sided.

"Give it some *slack*," she said.

"It's time to let your line out a little.

"Make sure there's enough *play* on the line. If there's too much tension, if the line begins to grow taut, it might snap or break. *Give it more play,*" she repeated. "Remember, there's a fish at the other end."

Sound advice. I plan to put on my to-do list:

More slack time.
Go fishing.

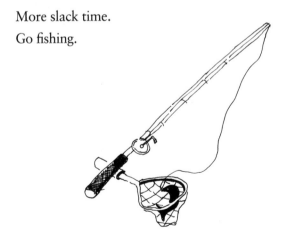

During this time, I went to the hospital for a biopsy, and they gave me an injection that left me alert, but not feeling the pain. All through the procedure I heard a loud, slow, definite THUMP, THUMP, THUMP.

Fascinated, wondering what this primal sound was doing in an operating arena, I asked the doctor, "What's that strange sound?"

"That's your heartbeat," he said.
"That couldn't be my heart," I said, sounding definite.
"I'm very fast."

"It is your heart," he answered. "Underneath your speedy behavior you have a strong and slow deeper rhythm."

As I was lying on the table, my attention was split, one part worrying about the results of the biopsy, another part wondering:

If I could learn to move from that strong and slow deeper rhythm, how would I move?

"Slowly, slowly—the smaller the movement, the bigger the change," Ofer said.

During that first Feldenkreis class with Ofer, he repeated these words several times. My pleasure in hearing them reminded me of the first time in Nancy's stretch class, soaking up a sweet and revolutionary message—"Practice enjoying. Don't practice struggling."

Listening, my body dropped down six octaves without my having to *do* anything. I had a glimpse of ease and thought of what Milan Kundera had said:

Why has the pleasure of slowness disappeared?

Anyone observing me with the pile of papers, folders, notes, and *miscellaneous* snippets that require two chairs by my side just to hold it all, because the table is small, would assume I'm just doing what I always do. On the surface that's true.

Two years worth of tiny pieces of paper has yielded seven pages of text. Is moving the pieces of paper around my way of avoiding the actual work? At the same time, I'm deeply involved and committed, absolutely certain I'm in the midst of writing again.

"Take your time," a friend said. "You're worth it.

"Hurrying cuts off feeling."

I remind myself of her words as I sit there each day. Absorbed, disappearing into the pages, I can feel an actual shift in attention. Time and judgment disappear. Hours later, when I stop, come up for air, return to regular time, I feel satisfied. I have been present.

I didn't struggle.

This is new behavior.

When I'm caught in struggle, I never feel satisfied. And I never feel I can stop. Working hard <u>all</u> the time is what I think I do. This has grown into such a firmly held belief that once when Mitzi heard, for the umpteenth time, my sorry tale of how hard I worked, with its twinge of the "poor me," she confused me by saying:

"Sue, I don't think you work hard enough."

"You *see* how hard I work! How can you say that?"

I could produce solid evidence, testimonials from a battalion of friends, saying how dedicated I was. But I sensed that Mitzi was onto something—and now I knew what it was.

Grappling is the word I used to describe this new way of working.

A wrestler, I learned, is called a grappler; it's a common sports term. When you're wrestling you have contact, a companion who responds. That's what it feels like to engage a problem and enjoy the contact. I had a partner when I was grappling; a bond was developing between the ideas, the writing, and me—in contrast to the loneliness of struggling.

Grappling is different from struggling. There is pleasure in the engagement. After four or five hours I not only feel satisfied, I know I could stop. Suddenly, I have choices. I can shift gears and do something else, or rest and relax. Or do nothing.

"When you *grapple* you engage a problem," Rachel said.

"When you *struggle* you engage a judge."

I let her words sink in. "To catch hold of something unseen and bring it to light," she added. "A perfect description of my writing process," I laughed.

I had just spent ten glorious days grappling—working with *vigor*.

For years, my deepest wish had been to get away from my world, in which I feel pulled in so many directions, and retreat to a silent space. A place free of distractions, to work nonstop on the zillions of pieces of paper I had collected. A place where someone else would cook dinner.

Do wishes come true if you wish hard enough?

I think the process is more complicated than that, but in September I left my home to spend a month at an artists' colony on a secluded ranch in northern California. Five nights a week we would be fed a delicious dinner. The rest of the time, the refrigerator would be stocked with supplies. And for one month, I would not have to get in a car.

On the second day of the retreat, eight lucky residents—three artists, two writers, a playwright, a composer, and a choreographer—gathered in the lounge for orientation. Some basic rules were explained: quiet during the day, dinner at seven. No TV or radio.

Then we each received a survivor's manual, a flashlight, and a whistle. For the next hour the leader briefed us on rattlesnakes (a rattlesnake can only strike as far as one-third of its length), poison oak, ticks, yellow jackets, and coyotes. A full-page instruction in the manual was entitled: IF YOU ENCOUNTER A MOUNTAIN LION.

"You can spot a mountain lion by its very large tail," the leader explained, and I wondered if that specific detail was necessary. My favorite mountain lion instruction:

Do all you can to appear larger.

Even paradise offers opportunities to stretch.

INVISIBLE WALL

Leah is a dancer, a poet of movement. We took a walk one of those first days at the colony, and as I watched how she carried herself, I wondered: I learn painting by copying the work of artists I admire—can I mimic her fluid motion, learn to be so alive in my body?

As we talked, she used the expression *invisible wall*. Intrigued, I asked her to say more. "It has to do with my work," she began. "I want to be involved and most times I am, but there are times when I'm very close to being engaged and then resistance comes up. The place that I am is not far from where I want to be, but there *is* a barrier—fixed and impenetrable—between me and my creative process."

"It's easy for me to imagine that wall," I said. "Sometimes I feel like the Energizer bunny, the one that keeps going and going and going on those TV commercials, bumping against the wall and continuing to bump. As I am bumping, I keep hoping that one of those times the wall will get tired, exasperated, or just bored enough to collapse. But the wall never moves. At those times, I am at a loss to come up with a new strategy to get over, around, or through it."

"If, instead of being an Energizer bunny, I make contact with the wall itself—get to know its characteristics, what it likes and what it doesn't—the wall will be less formidable. But at times, the wall is too much," Leah said, looking discouraged.

"At other times it's really flimsy," she continued, and when she's fully engaged in her work, stripped of her inhibitions, the wall is no longer there.

When Leah accepts the invisible wall—it softens.

By allowing the wall to exist, letting it be there just as it is, we find that something shifts. As we walked, Leah and I played with other ways to deal with a barrier—finding a hinge, a window, door, even a crack—even imagining the wall crumbling.

Could we learn to ignore it and behave *as if* we are in the work and, eventually, notice that we're actually there? Or like a cartoon character, draw a door on the wall, open it, and walk in?

I had spent that day writing about the terrible fall I'd had a few months earlier. I told Leah how I dealt with that trauma. To ward off feeling overwhelmed by what had happened, a part of me froze. She understood.

"I call the process of moving toward the wall *thawing*," she said.

When she starts a new work after a break, she says it feels like taking something out of the freezer. "It needs time to soften before I can really taste it and shape it. Once I have thawed, and embraced the project, there can be movement. That's where my work lives—that's where I live.

"But it's not the work that's taken out of the freezer—it's me."

A message in a box in a redwood stump left by one of the former residents read:

It's a slow thing to give strength to your song.

Many times there's a lag between what I hear and when I'm able to take the experience into my body. At the retreat, I chose never to get in a car. With no TV or radio, I loved and thrived on the silence.

Just before I had gone off, I had asked Nancy if there was a relationship between learning to move slowly and silence.

"The more you see how you generate your own noise, the more you can be open to silence," she had said. "If you can develop your silence, you see more clearly where you are—it's like having your windows cleaned."

The land at the retreat is very beautiful—and very steep. My "stretching lessons" left me unprepared for my first forty-five-minute uphill walk. I set out, trying to ignore the manual's warning about mountain lions, hoping it was a community joke. But climbing the hill was not a joke. It was hard work. My reward came around the third bend, where I saw a large yellow triangle-shaped sign that said:

Sometimes I'm too earnest in my seeking. I do trust my intuition, but yielding to whim seemed different—lighter, softer, more playful—even comic. I thought to myself:

"Add that to your repertoire!"

Leah had offered the image of an invisible wall that can get in our way. Then a letter arrived from my friend Donna, an American who lived in Japan with her husband and son, describing a space she had seen that existed between two real, concrete walls.

When she takes a walk in her neighborhood, she always notices a very modest, unattractive concrete housing project. A concrete wall surrounds it on two sides around a curve. The wall is ugly and too high to see over.

It has a space of about two inches of soil at the bottom where the wall meets yet more concrete that continues down all along the entire block. This tiny two-inch space of earth is planted with flowers.

The flowers are stunning—all colors, carefully planted, varying heights and kinds. The women change the flowers with the seasons and meticulously care for them.

The walk by this wall is like being in a mini-paradise.

These women were able to carve out a soft and tender expression between two hard spaces, all in this tiny, tiny space between two concrete walls. And they shared their *art* with everyone who passed.

They created beauty in the midst of severe limitation.

That space reminded me of how I had been in my body—the chrome machine, the rigid armor—and how I had begun to stretch and open to find the softness within. The *space between* that these Japanese women were able to create evoked all kinds of images. One was a quote from a famous pianist:

The notes I handle no better than many pianists, but the pauses between the notes—ah, that is where the art resides.

EAGLE VISION

I have always loved the myth of Psyche, the young woman who falls in love with Eros—especially when I learned that Psyche's name means *soul.*

Unfortunately, Psyche manages to incur the wrath of her jealous mother-in-law, Aphrodite, who makes her face a series of seemingly impossible tasks. If she can't complete them on time, the price will be death.

The one task I most identified with is to draw a single goblet of water from the river Styx, which is surrounded by treacherous terrain and guarded by monsters. Robert Johnson wrote, describing the challenge:

Feminine nature is flooded with the vastness of possibilities, and drawn to all of them.

As I read those lines, I knew he was describing the heart of my dilemma.

"I choose them all."

But Zeus's eagle comes to rescue Psyche. From high above, the eagle isn't caught in the "vastness of possibilities." Instead, it sees the panoramic view of the situation, chooses one spot, dives down, and retrieves the single goblet of water.

I now have a new practice. I call it EAGLE VISION.

I imagine myself soaring, like an eagle, above all the specific details of what is happening now. When my vision becomes larger, I notice things have a way of sorting themselves out.

From that place high above, I see clearly what <u>is</u> most important.

After all their trials and tests, Psyche is finally reunited with Eros. They have a child, which they name *Pleasure.*

In Greek, *psyche* means both "butterfly" and the human soul.

My husband often calls me a butterfly, without judgment, in fact with tenderness in his voice. Flapping my wings to avoid being caught is quite a different rhythm than what a butterfly does, but the movement of the butterfly is still something for me to aim for. Its job is to go from flower to flower, pursuing its own pleasure, finding refreshment where it can in the nectar of the flower, pausing, and then carrying out a bigger task—pollinating plants.

Later, I learned that a caterpillar, in order to become a butterfly, must absolutely wiggle itself out of a very, very tight skin. I added to my list of inquiries: the characteristics of butterflies. So far I've learned the ancients used the phrase *flying souls* for butterflies.

Slender threads, unexpected and mysterious connections.

Pay attention to what is beginning to awake within you.
The caterpillar can feel the essence of the butterfly even before it
begins to emerge.   DORIAN BIETZ

I spent more than a year reliving the meeting with Pamela and the sensation of goose bumps. I knew I had glimpsed something very large. At the same time, one part of me still wanted a logical explanation.

I was also waiting, not always patiently, for just the right moment to write to my friends, planning to ask them if they knew anything about goose bumps or if they had any experiences that gave them goose bumps.

A letter arrived from Switzerland from a woman I didn't know, named Susan, whose friend had forwarded my letter.

Goose bumps? Yes, I too pay attention to them. When I read your letter my arms were covered with shivering little bumps— the telltale sign for me that something is happening.

Plato spoke of goose bumps as vestiges of long ago, when our souls were seen as having wings. Plato believed that the openings from which the wings had to grow were rigid and closed at first, preventing them from shooting forth. But slowly, with love and care and patience, the rigid part melts—and the soul begins to grow wings.

Is that not wonderful?

Let us grow wings together.

As I read the words of a stranger, I felt goose bumps.

I scribbled *Let us grow wings* on a piece of paper. As I wrote the words, I saw that at the beginning of any new challenge we encounter obstacles, confusion, and doubts. That's natural. But when we allow the rigidity within us to begin to melt, we allow our soul to grow. I took a very deep breath and with eagle vision saw, that's what this journey is about.

We're inviting our soul to grow wings.

RISKING

What gets in our way—keeps us afraid to grow our wings?

OVERCOMING FEAR

"My heart's desire is to go away and write," I told a friend. Memories of silence were still with me, within me, from the time I had spent at the artists' colony.

"Where would you like to go?" Mitzi asked.

"I could go to a friend's house in Sonoma for two days and perhaps stay with another friend for two more days. But that wouldn't be a block of uninterrupted time."

"What about a hotel?" she suggested, trying hard to be helpful.

"A hotel for three weeks would be way too expensive."

I heard her suggestions and heard myself shoot them down, one by one. I heard and *felt* how stuck I was—caught in a cage I had designed for myself.

That same afternoon I happened to call Alev, a writer and friend who lives in San Francisco, with a question about publishing. Unexpectedly, I asked if she, from her vast network of friends, knew anyone to ask or anyplace I might go to rent a space, not too far away, for three weeks.

"Robert and I will be away for three weeks in October," she said. "Would you like to stay here?"

A dream answered.

I had been told that Alev had a wonderful writing room, and I was thrilled to be in San Francisco.

Grace? It certainly was good fortune.

Busy imagining my new writing life, I hardly heard her mention her beloved old cats, Blackie and Blue. My "job" would be to take care of them. My heart sank. I'm not a cat person. I like petting them if they are friendly, but I've never had a cat and don't feel particularly natural around them. Caring for cats felt like too much of a stretch—I was fearful.

What if they got out of the house while I was in charge?
What if they got sick on my watch?

Disappointment.

Another NO.

I told Mitzi of my chance opportunity, and she agreed. "Cats are so sudden in their movements," she said. "I never know where they're going to be."

I decided to *pause*. I'd think about what to do for two days.

Living with "NO" for two days felt terrible.

On the third day, I asked Alev, "Could I come over and say hello to the cats?"

Blackie and Blue were large—very large—old cats. Blackie was particularly enormous. Both had smooth, silky fur and exuded a sense of well-being. These cats *knew* they were dearly loved.

Alev showed me around the house, demonstrated how to pick the cats up, and explained that the cat door happened to be in the bedroom where I would be sleeping, so they would be going in and out when they felt like it. Or at night, if I preferred, I could carry them down the narrowest of narrow black metal staircases to the basement. In the morning I could let them out. She explained about food for the cats, fuse boxes, and which day to take the garbage out.

Her writing room was lovely. A magic place tucked in downstairs, with a view of a small garden.

Every corner and crevice in her home had objects and books, books, books, and there were many rugs. The objects themselves breathed history. Alev's house was full in every sense—the opposite of mine. Mine becomes full and alive when I'm able to create more and more empty space. I promised to call her in twenty-four hours.

When I got home, I called Mitzi to say I had been to see two very impressive cats. She'd been thinking about her initial response to cats and remembered, "Once I got contact lenses and could see them, I wasn't scared."

How much fear comes from not seeing, not knowing?

Next, I called Harriet, a friend and veterinarian, to ask her advice.

You can learn about *ease* and *pleasure* observing those cats," Harriet said. "They'll be wonderful teachers."

Immediately after telling Alev I would love to house-sit, take care of her cats, and write, out of nowhere a radiating pain from a pinched nerve in my hip appeared. The pain said, "NO." Determined to not break my word and believing Ofer would help make my hip better, I called him, asking if I could possibly have a private session—*immediately*.

I hardly ever drive in the dark, but the only time he could see me immediately was at 7:15 the next morning in Walnut Creek, almost an hour's drive from my home. And the freeway to Walnut Creek is infamous for the most Byzantine construction in the Bay Area: irrational overpasses, ever-changing exit signs—a horror even in daytime. I always hold my breath when I change lanes.

These obstacles loomed large.

Lots of "no's" have been a part of my vocabulary.

No driving at night.
No driving on freeways unless I really have to.
No good at following instructions.

The "no's" were not as important as the bigger "yes."

It was still dark when I set out for Walnut Creek at 5:45 A.M.; the exit markers would be even harder to find. Would the light come up by the time of the appointment? Ofer said I should watch out for 680 South, then immediately get into the left-hand lane, but he didn't say which side of the road the exit sign was going to be on. Even at that early hour, traffic was heavy, and I had no strategy to choose which of the four lanes to maneuver into.

Every once in a while I had to remind myself to breathe.

I saw signs up ahead, but still couldn't read them, and as I got close I was concerned about changing lanes at the last moment. I looked back, and suddenly there were no cars behind me. It was like Moses "parting the waters." I had time to breathe and get into the correct lane.

There are all kinds of miracles.

Relieved and grateful, I believed my problems were over.

I turned left immediately at the bottom of the ramp, and then went to make another left-hand turn as instructed. Bewildered, I saw two roads sharply to the left. I decided to follow the van in front of me.

The next thing I knew I was on a bumpy, steep dirt road surrounded by large cranes doing what large cranes do. A science fiction landscape: unfinished freeways overhead, in the dark, on a road that wasn't a road.

"Lady, you shouldn't be here," the crane driver shouted.

DANGER !

I knew that.

I was dreading the thought of getting on a different freeway, this time without instructions, but the crane driver turned out to be a good Samaritan and described how to find my way back down the bumpy terrain to the *other* left-hand street.

My need and my will had combined to overcome obstacles that had ruled me for a very long time. I arrived on time. I felt wonderful getting there, but there's a bigger lesson I learned, one I hope to remember:

Not to risk can also be a risk.

The door closed, and I was alone with Alev's cats, Blackie and Blue. A whoosh of fear came over me. What was I most afraid of? Alev had said they were old and slow cats. Would they get sick in my care—even die? Would they bolt out the front door as I went for a walk? Would they be so homesick for their beloved parents they would refuse to eat? Would one of them sense my nervousness when I went to pick him up and scratch me?

Before going down to the writing room, I had a talk with Blackie and Blue. I told them I was new at this and asked them to be patient with me. The first day and night they ate and slept and went out and came in. I let them know how happy I was to be in their home and how eager I was to write. When I gingerly stroked them, they seemed content, even welcoming. Relaxed and grateful, I felt things were going well.

On the third day, when I was ready to close up shop for the night, I called Blue to come in. No Blue. I went into the garden in the back, which I had thought was a safe, walled space. "Blue, Blue," I called. "Time to come in." I called, waited, called and rattled the treats, and finally beseeched: "*Please* come in. I want you to be safe. And I'd like a good night's sleep."

No Blue.

I had trouble sleeping that night. I kept getting up to go out to call Blue, rattling his treats. After only a few hours sleep, I was eager to get up and start my vigil. I dreaded looking in the garden, fearing I'd find a wounded cat. Later in the day, on the outside staircase leading to the street, I found his collar with his name tag, but no Blue.

That very long day, through sheer willpower, I wrote, went out for a cappuccino, stopped at the neighborhood pet store for advice, searched again, and returned to find Blue acting as if nothing unusual had happened.

I changed from being a worried cat-sitter to a keen observer of cats.

Blue was the adventurous one outside, often having to be called home for the night. Inside, Blackie was more aggressive. When treats were offered, Blackie immediately gobbled up first his, then Blue's share. Blue seemed resigned to his territorial fate, but I wanted equality.

Each morning I found them nestled together in a large leather dining-room chair, a sight to warm a mother's heart. I began to relax again. I had learned their routine, and they had learned mine. Then, after five days, they switched chairs.

Now they nestled on top of all the mail that had accumulated in a wicker basket at the front door. They changed their favorite sleeping spot five times while I was there. Experts at paying attention to their desires, they did not know the meaning of routine.

Twice Blue came home without his identification collar. Twice I went to the pet store to buy a new one, always chatting with the woman in charge. "You are so conscientious," the woman said on my third visit. "I'd be happy to give your name to some of my clients. They often come into the store asking if I know any professional cat-sitters."

"Sue, the cat expert," I laughed.

Expecting to work alone, I ended up with two unlikely teachers.

Endlessly watching the sensuous way they stretched—languid, taking their time—I realized I had always been cut off from that part of myself. They loved being stroked, and I loved stroking them, listening to them purr with unbounded contentment. Blackie and Blue modeled *bliss,* a word I don't often use—an experience I don't often have.

Sleeping in the sunshine on the deck, they surrendered totally to bliss, but were alert in an instant at the tiniest sound. And I imagined they liked watching me, a novice, thinking how funny I was, expecting I could lure them when they did not intend to be lured.

They embodied *presence*. From objects of worry, Blackie and Blue became worthy companions—and very fine teachers.

And most important, I learned to love them.

I'm a black-and-white person who wears black-and-white clothes and makes black-and-white handmade crooked ceramics," I say if anyone asks me to describe myself. Recently I've added gray to my list. And when I do hunger for a bit of color, I choose red.

My limited palette is familiar and safe. And I don't have to think too much about what to put on.

My body rhythm also seems to be more comfortable with extremes. It has only two positions, *off* and *on*. The off switch only operates when I finally stop flapping and go to sleep. There is no setting for rest. Yvonne mentioned a *dimmer* switch. I didn't know what that was.

"The dimmer switch is the alternative to the light switch that has only off and on," she said. "The dimmer allows you to have a whole range—from very bright light to very low, almost off, but not quite off."

The image of a dimmer switch with many more settings made me think of Nancy, who always encourages us to pick up some other channels—emotional, kinesthetic, sensory, rational. "Too much is happening on one channel," she says, and for me, I'm sure it's the thinking channel.

"Change your frequency. Increase your range."

TAKING A CHANCE

Could I build new habits—increase my range?

When I didn't get the Best Character award when I was twelve years old, an almost unbearable disappointment at the time, I had protected myself by refusing to compete, withdrawing into a smaller shell. Wearing so much armor had made me feel fragile underneath all the protection.

When I married, and Richard and I played tennis, I would never play "games." That was my rule. We would rally and I enjoyed playing, but I continued refusing to compete.

I almost never went to my son Michael's water polo games or to my son David's races when he was on the Berkeley High crew. I did go once, when they were competing for the championship against Redwood City. I couldn't breathe, could hardly bear to watch, and thought I would die from anxiety.

My reaction was so extreme that I finally persuaded myself to face this fear of competition. I would grow a new habit. As my first practice, I signed up for a tennis competition. The match was at 8:00 on a cold, dark morning, and though I almost never perspire, sweat poured out of me. I kept chanting to myself, "This is a brave thing to do," as I wondered whether I would survive the match.

I did win the first match, but winning was the least important part of the challenge. I just needed to do it—the price for not risking had become too high.

Facing fear that had ruled me since I was twelve, I had already won.

Years later, I entered one of my ceramics in a juried art show. Though I'd done this a few times before, I had always kept it a secret—even from Richard. This time, I told him and several friends.

How fragile is the shell—or the self inside that shell?

When the letter came announcing that my piece was rejected, I cried for a moment. Then I told Richard and friends my news. Disappointing, yes, but the fear of being disappointed wasn't worth all the good energy I had spent protecting myself. Something inside was already different.

Risking was worth it, no matter the outcome.

Now I had other choices—other ways to respond to life's possible disappointments and challenges. A year later, I applied to another juried show and was accepted. I was pleased to be accepted, but letting myself be seen—by myself and others, was the real triumph—whether I was accepted or not. I felt as if I had stretched a muscle.

I was no longer afraid of being seen.

You must do the thing you think you cannot do.
ELEANOR ROOSEVELT

M. C. Richards is a heroine of mine.

I still have my copy of her book *Centering,* first published in 1962, with many, many paragraphs marked in red with lots of *****. This was before I stopped marking up books that I love. Ceramics, paintings, and poetry, all fresh, bursting with life—she seemed unafraid to take on *whatever.*

Five years ago, at my local bookstore, I happened to glance down below the counter and I noticed a purple flyer announcing a six-week workshop she was teaching: "Clay, Color, and Word." I rushed home, called, and signed up.

When I arrived at the first class, there was a tall, slim, gray-haired woman with a handsome, weathered face—M. C., seventy-seven years old—a formidable presence.

We immediately connected and began meeting in between classes. She told me how thrilled she was that her first class went so well.

"Why is it I suffer so much beforehand?" she asked. "I'm apprehensive, insecure, and anxious." Then, when the moment comes to begin, she stands on her feet or sits on a high stool, and everything comes together.

"What happens? What is this thing that is *called forth?*"

"It's a collaborative dance," I said.

She agreed. She puts herself in relationship with the others in the room—their response comes, and then she carries on. "I have to give up control as I enter the dance with the other."

"We can't script what others will say," she added. "We can't know in advance—until we do it together.

"They're calling forth something in me—teacher, poet, clown.

"And I'm responding. A different part of myself responds, not the *small* me that was having difficulty and feeling insecure. The group, together, this inner relationship is yeast, mystery, and creativity. It's in everybody's domain. Mutually they feel it—then the ball isn't always in my court." Then she adds, as if speaking to all of us:

"Something in you will be *called forth*. Trust it."

Nancy's class at the studio had always been called "Just Stretch." One day I noticed it had been renamed: "Undercurrents."

Odd, I thought. How would anyone know what the class was about? Although by then I would have joined any class she was teaching—even if it was labeled "Green Cheese." I asked her what the new title meant.

"*Undercurrents*—that's what's under our need to accomplish anything," she said.

"It's what's underneath our patterns, under all our activity.
"It's what's underneath our need to seek anything.
"It's what's underneath our need to fix ourselves in some way."

To hear her tell me that there is nothing more to prove, nothing to be done, makes me want to cry with relief. I imagine getting off my treadmill of effort as she says: "Practice feeling good where you are.

"Stretch into all the places you haven't yet lived in yourself."

"*Let yourself have more of yourself.*"

In the past, when asked to do something that seemed too much of a stretch, I never thought to say "NO." When I was invited to be on a religious panel at the American Booksellers Convention in Chicago, I was pleased and honored. Then I took a second look and called the man back. "I don't think I'd be good on a panel." "Oh, no," he assured me. "We think you'll do fine."

I <u>never</u> thought to say "NO."

While writing *Everyday Sacred,* the image of the begging bowl came into my life. Since then I've been doing this dance: when I feel I am being asked to do something that is too much of a stretch, I speak up. If those on the other end don't back down— and so far they never have—I tell myself:

"Something unexpected has been placed in my bowl. There must be some spirit reason I'm being asked to do this. I may not understand what that is right now, but I will do my best to suspend judgment."

Then I say "YES."

For the next two months I was overcome by an even larger than usual dose of fear and doubt, especially when I heard that my publisher would be in the audience. "I'll let him down," I worried, a familiar feeling in my body from long ago. "He'll see me fail."

In between worrying, I did spend a great deal of time actually working on my presentation.

When I got to Chicago, a city I love, instead of enjoying the sights in my free time, I stayed in the room, practicing and timing myself, since I had no idea how much one can say in ten minutes. One sound piece of advice came from Yvonne:

"The first way to be on a panel is to *listen.*"

When the program was over, I had survived. The talk had gone well.

"A triumph," someone said.

There was a happy ending—but it came in a form I wasn't expecting. I saw, as if for the first time, that if this is the behavior I have to go though to get these positive results, the price is too high.

I had another choice—one I had never considered before.

The next time I'm asked to do something that feels particularly stressful, I can say, "I'm very flattered to be asked, but, NO, I'm not taking on that kind of challenge right now." I am not, after all, a monk. My bowl doesn't have to be open to receive <u>all</u> the time.

Symbolically, I can turn my bowl over.

There are times when it is a strength to move inward—to trust oneself enough not to push out there in the world by sheer will or effort. And there are other times when taking on something difficult can be a worthwhile stretch.

Once I give myself permission to say "NO," I can imagine saying "YES" with less effort and more trust.

How will we know how far we can stretch if we don't try?

YES!

When Audio Renaissance asked me to read *Plain and Simple* and *Everyday Sacred* on tape, I was thrilled. "YES!" I said with no hesitation. A new challenge—one that would last a week.

The recording was to be done at Fantasy Records, a state-of-the art recording studio in Berkeley, whose entryway proudly displays the platinum records they have earned. Sitting on a high stool, looking through a glass wall at the director, the engineer, and banks of technical equipment, I imagined myself a rock star exuding confidence. But the reality was that the first day was much harder than I had expected.

Every other minute, the director asked me to stop and repeat what I had just said. Either they heard me breathing, or the sound of a single page of text dropping to the floor was too noisy, or my pace or rhythm wasn't just right. By the end of that first day, we had only gotten though twelve pages, and we had two books to complete by Friday evening.

"I don't think I'm good at this kind of storytelling," I told my son David that night.

"One of the fondest things I remember about Grandma," he responded, "is how much I loved how she read stories to me. I always looked forward to it."

I took his words in, really heard what he had to say. I took a deep breath and felt those famous indicators, my shoulders, which are often up close to my ears, drop down as I thought,

"Maybe I <u>am</u> my mother's daughter."

The next morning, I read from my heart, envisioning the way my mother might have read.

"What happened last night?" the director asked. "You are so much more at ease."

Often, while looking for something, we find something else, far more valuable.

We come home—full circle.

Running around in circles, the full moon, healing circles, the fact that no two people can draw exactly the same circle—are all reasons why the image of the circle intrigues me.

"You should call Kaz," a friend said, when I mentioned this fascination. "He knows all about circles." "I'll be happy to talk to you," Kaz said when I called. "Come over."

Why do we sometimes procrastinate endlessly over something, and sometimes just do it?

When Kaz and I met at his front door we knew nothing about each other. He was about sixty, slim, with a face that was calm but intense, and he wore a black robe like a monk's. On his walls were glorious circles—bold, audacious strokes in deep, rich black ink.

Over tea, I learned that he was a calligrapher, a calligraphy teacher for forty-five years, the author of many books, and a translator of classical Buddhist texts. As we talked, I saw he was *bigger than that*—a very special spirit.

I learned later, from others, that he is in fact a world-renowned calligrapher. The circles he draws are called *enso* in the Japanese Buddhist tradition. A Zen circle, Kaz explained, is an expression of enlightenment—"an experience of completeness." Every time it is drawn with a brush it is *unique* for each individual, for each moment.

When Suskai Roshi, a great Zen teacher and one of Kaz's teachers, was about to die, his students gathered around and asked, "Where do we meet?" He drew a circle, bowed, and died.

For the next two and a half years I daydreamed about circles. I fed my dreams on one of Kaz's books—circles and brushstrokes that felt like fresh mind on paper. Then, during one of my constricted phases—writing from the knuckles down, I call it—a friend who is psychic said she saw my third chakra—my creativity—as the size of a very small walnut.

At the same time, I heard that Kaz would be teaching a class on Sunday afternoon. That will free me up, I thought, teach me more about circles, and maybe help the walnut to grow. The students— twenty of us, each had our own small, felt-covered bridge table, with a brush, an ink stone, and a pile of white paper. I couldn't wait to pick up the thick brush.

I imagined myself drawing circles with great abandon.

As Kaz began talking, I realized what I had signed up for was a class in classical Japanese calligraphy. We were to copy classic strokes, as precisely as we could, from a page in front of us. So much for wild abandon!

"I think I am getting worse," I said halfway through the class, showing Kaz the brushstroke I had just made.

"How can you get worse at the beginning?" he asked.

He addressed the question to the group, and then came over to my table. "Let me help you," he said. My arm froze as he put his hand over mine and I tried to follow along. I spent a long afternoon trying hard to be a good student. Happily, we took several breaks. As I was leaving, he said, "I have an invitation for you."

The invitation was to another class, a small, informal calligraphy group that met at his home once a month, very flexible. "Would you like to come?"

"I would be honored," I said.

I still wasn't interested in calligraphy; I was interested in being with Kaz, who, in his quiet way, had a *presence*—which reminded me of M. C. I have come to treasure our small group. And I am still probably one of the most inept students he has ever taught, though his mind is not bogged down by petty comparisons.

We do classical calligraphy, but after a period of faithfully copying the Japanese character, I give myself permission to take a break, and draw circles with abandon.

"Could I include some of your brushstrokes in *Stretching Lessons?*" I asked Kaz.

"No. I think you should make them."

I was about to say no, till I thought back to "We must do the thing we think we cannot do."

I offer a beginner's beginner brushstrokes.

I've been going to Nancy's stretching classes now for three years, so some of the faces are familiar. A year ago I noticed a startling change in the one of the "regulars." He walked slowly, haltingly, as if in a daze, with a faraway look on his face. He was unable to speak or go to class.

"What happened to Gene?" I asked Nancy. I learned he had suffered a horrendous stroke and had lost most of his "thinking" power. One side of his body was paralyzed. He was not expected to live very long.

As months went by, I saw Gene improve. Though his walk was still tentative, the change was remarkable. "Gene, it's wonderful to see you getting stronger," I said one day, thinking he might finally understand what I was saying.

"Yes," he acknowledged, a tremor in his voice.

Six months later Gene returned to Nancy's class. He came up to me afterward, and said, "Did you know I almost died? All the doctors thought I would be dead three months after my stroke."

He had been in the hospital, unconscious, for many weeks, and when he regained consciousness, he couldn't understand or believe what had happened to him. He was sent to rehabilitation, where a physical therapist started by teaching him how to brush his teeth.

At first, the therapist brushed his teeth for him, but eventually he relearned the task.

"They taught me at forty-eight how to brush my teeth," he said. "And now I do it better than I did before." He smiled triumphantly.

"I'm the Michael Jordan of brushing my teeth!"

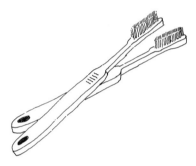

Next, they taught him to comb his hair and put on his pants. When the therapist pointed to the pants and asked what they were, he looked at them, puzzled. He really didn't know. The therapist offered four suggestions. He picked *eyebrow*.

"Before my stroke, my bright mind was going too fast—missing the details." Now he could think of only one thing at a time. No extra thoughts interfered with what he was doing. "Now my mind is slower than before." Sounding confident and pleased, he added, "I'm retraining myself—and I'm better at some things now than I ever was before.

"No past, no concern about the future, only the present.

"I've been given a second chance!"

Slow motion gets you there quicker.   HOAGY CARMICHAEL

What would happen if I changed my routine?

Nancy often says we only get good at what we practice. Nothing changes if we never do anything different. Unless we explore what is unfamiliar, we won't find new *space*—in our day, in our bodies, and in our lives.

What if, instead of starting my day reading a page in each of five spirit books, then taking an early morning walk, and after that going to Café Milano to write, I started my day working at home for three hours, from 6:00 to 9:00 A.M.?

Then, like a child who needs a reward for giving up her favorite toy, in this case my familiar groove, I'd go to an aerobics class at 9:45.

"Heartwork" the class is called.

It's taught by a terrific, lively instructor, who is supportive even when I go off in the wrong direction. Halfway through the class, she fell.

"Don't worry," she cried, tears running down her face. "I'll be fine in ten minutes."

Clearly in pain, she bravely continued reassuring us. "I'm a dancer. I know how to *push through* these things."

I'm sure she does know her body. But I could also see she had experienced a shock—her body had sustained a trauma. Various women offered assistance: one called for ice, another offered to go home and get an Ace bandage, and another suggested putting wet towels on her ankle. I sat next to her, holding her hand, and in a very gentle, soothing voice encouraged her, "Don't be in a hurry to get up."

"The quieter you allow your body to be, and the slower you move, the more rest you can take in—the quicker you will heal." I said this softly, backed by the great clarity of what I was learning.

"Listen to what your body is telling you."

"Are you a doctor?" someone asked.

I was telling her things I *know*, but know I don't do for myself.

Next time something happens to me, I <u>will</u> hear my own calm voice and listen to my own good advice.

"Show me how you sit when you work at the computer," Ofer said to a new client. She had come because she had severe back pain, and nothing she was doing seemed to help. Her posture looked quite good. After observing her for a while, he suggested she experiment. "Could you sit improperly?" he asked.

She resisted. Proud of her erect posture, it was hard for her to even imagine another way of sitting. Finally, she did begin trying new positions. When she slouched in the chair, she noticed her back pain went away. When she sat properly again, within a minute the pain returned. Now she had a choice. Not wishing to look crooked, she chose to sit up straight—with pain.

Thinking about the <u>right</u> thing to do often gets in the way of doing it right.

Ofer told me of a wealthy client of his who had more than enough money to buy the car he wanted. But he had a conflict between what he wanted and what he would allow himself. He couldn't bring himself to buy the handsome car.

After their first session together, Ofer gave his client a homework assignment. "Go to the drugstore and look at all the toothbrushes," he said. "There's an enormous choice of toothbrushes. Look at all of them. Then pick the one that most appeals to you, the one *you* want, regardless of price."

Ofer knew that the price difference between toothbrushes is small, and for most people the task of choosing would be relatively easy. So the key to change for this client was to move to a level of ease.

"Decrease the demand."

"Do you think people can change?" I asked.

"When we learn that the process of change is not only <u>not</u> difficult, but can actually be easy and enjoyable—change can happen rapidly," he answered.

"Once change becomes a joyful process, the fear of change disappears. And with it, most of the difficulties."

Ofer had us do a simple movement in class, gently moving our toes with our hands—a nonthreatening lesson. Halfway through the class, holding my right foot up toward my chest, I suddenly remembered a visit I had with a physical therapist. I went because I had a pain in my neck—this was years before I started stretching to learn more about spirit through my body. After several sessions, he commented:

"Sue, you have three-year-old feet."

I never stopped to ask what he actually meant. Silently I wondered, "How long do you think I will have to work with you to have feet that match my age?" I *felt* his pronouncement was a prophecy of doom. I never went back to the therapist.

After class, I asked Ofer about my three-year-old feet. "What does that mean?" he asked, repeating my question. "You sound as if you thought it was bad to have three-year-old feet. When I think of three-year-old feet," he continued, "I see them as *pliable*. I think they serve their owner better than fifty-year-old feet."

Now, all these years later, I'm getting to know those three-year-old feet and that three-year-old person who belongs to the feet.

And I'm not tripping over my own feet so much.

I still go to an aerobics class once a week, on Sundays. I'm not sure if it's wise or stupid to jump up and down on a recuperating Achilles tendon and an occasionally radiating hip. Each week the teacher changes and the people who come are a "mixed assortment" of sizes, ages, and shapes, but we're all low-key fitness types who choose not to take it easy on Sunday morning.

"What do you usually do in class?" the new instructor—a young man—asked.

"It's an easy class," I assured him. "Very low-key."

As I spoke, in marched twelve extremely tall golden Amazons—looking like Venus and Serena Williams or younger sisters of Arnold Schwarzenegger—radiating health and fitness. "Is this the kickboxing class?" they asked with great enthusiasm.

"Yes," he said, relieved.

In that moment of "yes," I almost bolted.

But, to my surprise, I found my body still in place as he turned on the music. We began with leg movements that were like a boxer's, then shifted to a routine with one fist held in front of the face.

"I don't want to see faces, just fists," he instructed.

Next came jabs. Then quickly he had us launch into uppercuts, punch and duck, right hooks, and later a left-right-left-duck routine. I wished my sons could have seen me, thinking how amused they would be at the sight of their mother as we moved into kicks, then a more complex routine of left kick, left jab.

Enjoying the beat of the music, I noticed with surprise that the fancy footwork was easy to follow. I didn't even drop out as I usually do during partner exercises. We were given an object that was like an oversized Ping-Pong paddle with soft padding in the middle.

I faced one of the Amazons, thinking the only thing we had in common was our height, and volunteered to go first. My job was to do the jab-punch combination we had just learned, connecting my fist with my partner's paddle. I also had to remember the fancy footwork.

This required *focus*.

I was thrilled when my fist found and gently connected with the paddle. I was unsure who or what I imagined punching, but delighted with this unexpected way of getting aggression out. We then switched positions and I was holding the paddle. My partner did her one-two punch and hit the paddle with tremendous force, leaving my knees feeling shaky.

A knockout punch, I thought.

"You were terrific," my Amazon partner said when we were finished. Was this drama part of my natural rhythm?

I have usually loved the classes that stressed *slow* and *gentle*. Now I thought of Nancy, who often reminds us, "The more aspects of yourself you can feel, the more options you have, the more power you can draw from." That Sunday morning my body knew what her words had been saying. I felt a new kinship with those towering Amazons.

"I choose them all," I laughed.

PARADOX

Does a warrior go out hunting for calm?

What supplies does she take for the adventure?

When I confided to Mitzi how delicious it was to think I could change and have more calm and ease in my life, with an innocent smile she said:

"I think you want more excitement!"

These two notions seemed so clearly and completely opposed that I laughed, realizing she was probably right. Once I understood that BOTH were true, gentle stretches <u>and</u> kickboxing, calm <u>and</u> excitement, I felt more spacious—outgrowing my old shell.

I'll never settle easily for calm, although I continue to long for it. Challenge and struggle are too much a part of my nature. Calm is exciting because it's a tender new feeling. What I want is *both*. More excitement and more calm. "To be calm and to excite my heart."

"CHOOSE A PROGRAM," the exercise machine commanded in bouncing red letters. Smiling, I think even at 5:45 A.M. a machine brings me a message.

"IT IS IMPORTANT TO CHOOSE BEFORE YOU BEGIN," it states.

I had lots of choices: *Walk in the Park*, *Steady Climb*, *Vail Pass*, and *Himalayan Trek*. I pick *Walk in the Park* and notice a heavy-set woman, whom I've often seen but never spoken to, on the machine next to mine. Usually I mind my own business, but this morning I ask, "What program did you pick?" *"Himalayan Trek,"* she said, smiling.

"Then nothing will daunt me the rest of the day."

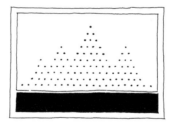

"Ease is hard, Sue," Mitzi said one day with a wry smile.

"I mean hard to come by." And then she gently poked me a little more. "Is it true that ease, like miracles, comes only after hard work?"

I didn't answer. But I trusted my desire to grow new behavior.

"I applaud your intention," Mitzi continued. "Ideally your method of change should be like the result you seek—*ease-y.*"

Mitzi is right. When we're feeling overwhelmed and caught in our struggle, it's hard to see ourselves clearly—and even harder to see our path. *"Listen to the whispers,"* Nancy had said. Perhaps our first steps could be gentle, small, and as soft as a whisper.

Because of my long history as an "expert" at struggle and effort, I can say with confidence: the pressure to succeed usually produces the opposite results. We don't have to be experts to start moving gently toward new behavior—and seeing ourselves differently.

When we move in the right direction—success is already there.

I'm a hideous typist. Anyone who has ever received a letter from me would agree. Although I type words, they never appear in the correct order, and often the letters are not the letters I meant to type, so I spend a great deal of time struggling to decipher what I have just written and struggling to figure out what I must have meant. Then I redo and redo the work, until it gets to be readable.

I am resigned to my fate.

But I still don't take responsibility. The reason for this handicap is *out there* I tell myself—a condition I was born with. I label it: dyslexic.

Years ago, before computers came in to do some of the work for us, I volunteered one day a week to work for an organization I believed in. My assignment that first day was to type a pile of letters. I warned them I was a terrible typist. I suggested they give me another task—*anything*. They would hear none of it.

There were times that day when I looked at the page and thought "pretty good." I would give it a *pass*. But the person in charge didn't agree and sent me back to start all over again. This back-and-forth dance continued throughout the day—until I finally got it right. I had spent one full day correcting and recorrecting a one-page letter—an important lesson in patience and humility.

Sometimes, change is a matter of *intention* and *attention*.

Gene's new way of being present inspired me. After years of accepting the fact that I was an awful typist, but blaming it on my label, dyslexic, I began to experiment. If I took more time, focused more on each word as I was typing, would I make fewer errors?

I took on typing as a *mindful practice*.

Would anything change?

Slowing myself down, paying more attention, I began to see correctly spelled words appear on the page. A small lesson in stretching—a *big* triumph!

Fifteen years ago, while writing *Plain and Simple,* I described myself as an *urban cockroach.* The image captured my endless scurrying, flapping my wings, frantically trying to get everything done on my totally unrealistic to-do list.

My editor, offended by the image, kept crossing the words out. I kept putting urban cockroach back in the text. When he announced, "I've finished editing," I tried once more. I never succeeded.

That image lingered until recently, when I helped Loie clean out her mother's apartment. Her mother was moving into a nursing home, and a group of friends joined forces to do the sad but necessary task. When we had finished, Loie, my role model and inspiration for being present and grounded, commented on how much I had gotten done with focused attention.

"You move with deliberate action."

Sometimes we stay stuck in our old pictures that describe how we were. We forget the changes we have made.

I no longer feel like a scurrying urban cockroach.

Acknowledging that I move quickly and deliberately is progress.

KNOWING OURSELVES

Often the way forward is through a detour.

SUSAN ROTHENBURG, ARTIST

Change doesn't move in a straight line—even though there are still many times I wish it would. I move forward, resist and regress, and then sometimes make what feels like a breakthrough. My learning path continues to be zigzag.

What gets in the way of our knowing ourselves?

I have an ongoing conversation with friends on the subject. "Many times I don't even know *what* I know," a friend told me, "at other times, in not saying what I know, I risk forgetting what I know."

"Doubting myself is so deeply ingrained," another friend added. "It's like getting layers of paint off an old oak door. Even when it's really well done, there are still a few places where the paint stays. Can you really remove it all?"

Right now she's feeling especially grounded, the doubt has receded, but she still has a habit of doubting herself in the language she uses, just because doubting is familiar. Like looking at the place on the wall where the clock used to be even though it's no longer there.

"These last years I feel I need to *be as big as I am*," another friend confided. "That's what I want," she said, sounding triumphant.

"But I've been afraid that if people see who I *really* am—then they will be mad at me." I told her that when I was a child my mother didn't yell at me often, but when she did her presence loomed large and fierce. I felt frightened and overwhelmed by her wrath.

"You have it so *easy*," she would shout, as if having it easy was a bad thing.

Trying to be someone else's idea of who we are makes us *smaller than*. If we can't speak what we know—without fearing the consequences—we are diminished. We can hide our **big**ness and magnificence out of fear of criticism and jealousy.

Yes, my friend agreed. "If I wasn't just serving my mother—if I was in my own magnificence—that would be dangerous." Then she added, grinning, "But I had an aunt who gave me a great gift, which I hold in my heart to this day:

"She saw the person I am—within the person I was."

When we allow ourselves to be more of who we are—it is a risk.

The form and style of risk-taking may differ—but *risks are risks.*

LABELS

Even before I went to live with the Amish, more than twenty years ago, I hated, truly hated, to go to a dinner or cocktail party and be asked:

"And what do you do?"

I knew I would be judged no matter how I answered.

My stomach would clench—a strong and immediate visceral
reaction. With the question came a hierarchy of labels, loaded with
points and comparisons—this is better than that—a consensus.
A friend said,

"Be careful what you put after 'I AM'. . . because you are."

Even now, when I have labels to declare, success to report,
I hate the question. I'm comfortable telling you this, but not as
comfortable letting you know there is a part of me that still wants
approval. That's only natural. But with certain people and in
certain situations my well-being, my sense of myself, is at stake
if I don't get that stamp of approval. I revert to being a needy
young girl, earnest, trying so hard to measure up to my father's
expectations.

Perhaps Pamela's story touched me so deeply because it was a
reminder—an antidote to labels. Each of us has something to give
and it is important to trust and value that—whatever it is.

I had been moving slowly, waiting and waiting for just the right time to write to Pamela, the woman who had said, "I'm not an artist. I have no talent." Early one morning reading in bed, I saw the words of Mother Teresa describing her work with the lepers in India:

Loneliness and the feeling of being unwanted is the most terrible poverty.

We won't let them grow hungry if we see their dignity.

Pamela sees the dignity of her homeless friends. Her *art* is caring.

How important it is for each of us to see our own dignity—our own worth. From that place, how much easier it is to see the dignity of others—their own worth.

Mother Teresa's words gave me just the right shove. I wrote to Pamela asking what she remembered of our conversation, nervous about what she might say. Our brief visit had meant so much to me. Might it have meant nothing to her?

Pamela wrote:

When we were together that evening at the YWCA, talking about talent and people being artists, I was remembering a gathering of friends years ago. We all sat around and decided what talent we had. One could play the piano, another could sing, and another was an incredible writer, somebody else could play the violin, and someone else could sew beautifully.

When my turn came, I thought to myself, "I can't even begin to match what they are saying." My friends stood around waiting for me to say something. Finally, one of them said, "The truth is, Pamela, you just don't have any talent."

"That's right," I finally conceded. And I just continued to go through life thinking I had no talent. My interpretation of an artist was much narrower than yours. So when you said, "Pamela, you are an artist," your words went to the very core of my being. I thought to myself, "What does she mean, I am an artist?"

Then I thought, "There are different ways of being an artist, and Sue has just paid me one of the highest compliments I have ever had." After our talk, I was at an art gallery and people were discussing artists, and I quietly smiled to myself and thought, "Art can be interpreted in so many different ways."

"I'm doing what I am meant to be doing," Pamela said.

"What we do with our lives makes us an artist."

STRETCHING

HEARTSONG

What does my heart know?

My heart knows HUGE.

My heart really knows. And though I often can't put words to it
and too often I don't listen—my heart is the best and wisest and
most consistent guide leading me. When I am desperate enough
(if only I didn't have to wait till then), my heart is my best teacher.

"ENOUGH," it shouts.

When my heart really hurts, full to bursting—I finally listen.

I continue to be very successful at <u>not</u> changing some of my habits.

After I fell on my head I tried my best to ignore the whole incident, to hold on to my routine by sheer willpower. To acknowledge that I was vulnerable, to be still and allow the healing process to take place was too hard, too much of a stretch.

A friend came by to see how I was feeling, and with great enthusiasm gave me a tape by the poet David Whyte. I was feeling exhausted, but after she left I began listening. He told of an adventure from his twenties, when he was strong and living a daring, adventurous life with "an invulnerable feeling about himself."

While walking in the Himalayas, he came upon a bridge over a huge chasm; one of the cables holding it up had collapsed, leaving huge gaps in the narrow walkway. He was standing, afraid to go forward, hoping the bridge might spontaneously repair itself, when an old woman with a large sack on her back approached.

"Namaste," she said and bowed.

In Sanskrit, namaste means:

"The spirit in me sees the spirit in you."

But, before he could lift his head to return her greeting, she shuffled across.

With that lovely greeting, I dozed off. I don't know how long I slept, but the next thing I heard was Whyte saying:

"Take pride in your limp."

I felt goose bumps. It didn't seem to matter that I had missed large pieces of the narrative: I never did find out what happened at the bridge. Somehow, the story didn't have to make sense. What I felt was *beyond* logic—I could see *deeper than that.*

I had been a limping warrior, denying my limp.

All my life I had feared being vulnerable. That was my limp. And I had done my best to protect myself against it. When I could accept my vulnerability as just another part of me—the thing I had feared most became a strength.

I confided about my new relationship with my limp to a friend. "Could you say the same thing about your need to struggle?" she asked.

"Struggling <u>is</u> my talent," I protested.

My resistance did not discourage her. "Could you say, 'I have struggling energy in me, but it is not me. I am not the struggle'?"

That I understood.

I can release some of that struggling energy when I make that distinction. I can keep reminding myself: I have struggling energy in me. But it is not me.

I am <u>not</u> the struggle.

RED SOCKS

Nancy was on vacation for several weeks. Her friend, Morning Star, began class by saying, "Flexible bodies make flexible minds." Then she continued:

"Let go of your agenda.
"Unravel your patterns—get to the sweetness under your drama."

I immediately relaxed.

The fall on my head and the radiating hip had been drama. Now she was suggesting we stretch *into* the places that are hurting or stiff. "Go in there and explore. Find out what your body likes."

One day, after class, I asked if she had any suggestions about my radiating hip. She said she would be happy to take a look, adding,

"I see with my eyes closed."

"There's almost no energy in your left hip," she announced. She saw my hip as a fractured spiral going backward, with the energy going the wrong way. "As a result, there are energetic stress marks." On a rational level I didn't understand what she was saying, and just as I was about to close down and dismiss her words as a lot of mumbo jumbo, she added,

"Energetically, there's been a *limp!*

"Energetically, you have been limping for quite a while."

I hadn't told her anything about my "limp theory of strength." She next asked if she could make a few gentle adjustments on my legs and around the hips. "Yes," I said, now feeling grateful and open to what she might do and see.

My hip did stop radiating after she worked on me. "Don't go back to wearing your old shoes," she advised. "If you stay in old shoes, you'll go back to your old ways."

The expression on my face must have told her I wasn't going to rush out and buy new shoes. "Even new socks would help," she offered.

"Red socks!" I said immediately.

The next day I went to Macy's and searched for the reddest red socks I could find. I have been wearing them ever since. "It takes twenty-one days to learn a new habit," she said, recommending I find a small, modest strategy—switching the silverware around, moving pictures—anything to remind me and my body that I was in the process of creating new patterns. As we stood at the door saying good-bye, she smiled and said:

"Our bodies don't respond well to ultimatums."

I laughed when I heard that. Not only is it funny; it's true.

After several weeks the radiating hip returned, but never as strong as before. When the hip does create a bit of drama, I ask myself:

"What is my hip trying to tell me? What does my spirit need?"

TALISMAN

"I <u>want</u> to overcome my need to struggle." I had told Rachel.

"People who write have developed all kind of ways to seduce the muse," she said. "They wear a certain sweater, use the same pen, write at the same time or place each day. Or they have a rabbit's foot nearby." Then, with a delicious twinkle in her eye, pointing to me, she said:

"You struggle. That's your rabbit's foot!"

At the time, I had agreed with her diagnosis. But now I have more possibilities—more range. I can choose another rabbit's foot—red socks.

I reported to M. C., feeling rather pleased with myself, that I had uncovered an old belief—a hidden assumption—that I needed to struggle and suffer in order to do good works and deeds.

Her response took me by surprise. "Even if you think you are being *called* to do something—and even if the goals you're striving for are worthy—that defeats the very thing you're after—a relief from striving."

Many people who I think are wise have told me that there is nothing I have to *do*—and nothing I have to prove. And when they say those words, I know they mean "all of us."

But whenever I hear that, I resist.

I'm not sure why I feel that's threatening, but the idea that I am fine just as I am goes against a core belief—that I must work hard all the time to get better. And no matter how evolved the person who says it is, I can feel in my body that I am coming up against my edge. I do not want to open and take the message in.

"Give yourself the freedom to be disappointed," M. C. continued, "and give others the freedom not to be interested in what you are doing.

"Give them the freedom not to love you."

"How blessed I am to have you as a friend," I told her, "even if I'm not ready to take that leap." She responded, "Give yourself the freedom to make your own relationship with yourself, instead of trying to choreograph it or trying to live up to an old self-image."

"Give yourself the ease to be who you are, the full octaves, not just the upper register—the full scale of yourself!"

SOMEDAY

On the radio, I heard a reporter describe a conversation he had with a seven-year-old girl wearing a sweatshirt with soccer star Mia Hamm's picture on it.

"Are you Mia Hamm?" he asked. The child looked puzzled. "Tell him," her mother said, encouraging her to speak up.

"Someday," she answered.

"Places explain people," a friend said, seeing me in my home.

Lately I've wished for order, inside and out, as a way to feel calm.

For thirty years, my family has lived in a large Spanish-style house in the Berkeley Hills. When we bought the house, Richard and I decided to have our bedroom downstairs, next to the living room. It was a lovely room with a view of trees, a tiny piece of the Golden Gate Bridge, and parts of Oakland and San Francisco in the distance. Originally, it had been a garage.

It had only one small, narrow closet.

For twenty-eight years I was content searching for my white blouses and black pants in the one crowded closet. In the dark, they all looked alike. Putting a new closet in our bedroom would have meant getting rid of a packed floor-to-ceiling bookcase, a fixture in the room—and would have diminished the spaciousness of the room. I kept bumping up against an invisible wall, without a glimmer of a creative solution.

For the last three years, a friend had been telling me, "Sue, you and Val should meet. You'd really like each other." Val and I met, by chance, in front of my house as I was saying good-bye to our mutual friend. She came to visit the next week.

I told Val about the closet impasse.

"If you like, I could look around for half an hour and make a few suggestions," she offered.

In that half hour she was optimistic that something could easily be worked out. My mood shifted dramatically—I felt I had received a transfusion—seven thousand volts of her boundless, creative, energy.

The next time she came, she brought a small black notebook. "Could I look around the house? Can I peek into your closets?" she asked. She took some measurements and, after an hour, asked, "What would you think of having your clothes in the closet in the living room?"

"The living room?"

The living-room closet, not very large, was already crammed with Richard's jackets, some of my clothes, old children's games, raincoats, records, books—a hodgepodge. Could I change my expectation that a clothes closet had to be in the bedroom? "And how would you feel about giving Richard your closet in the bedroom?"

I did not want to give up anything.

Nothing changes if we never do anything different, I reminded myself, and then said "yes" to both suggestions.

On her next visit she arrived with a batch of white hangers, the kind you get at your supermarket—a dollar a dozen. Then came the hardest part. Everything I owned had to fit in that closet. And I had to be able to see each thing.

She was a strict taskmaster. By most people's standards, I have few clothes and don't mind wearing them over and over again, year after year. But the small living-room closet would still be crammed if I kept them all.

When I could think of a friend who would enjoy something, it was easy. Finally, I had to trust that the person at Goodwill would be just the right person to receive my things.

I saw my goal.

I had a clear intention.

We painted the dark wood closet the whitest of whites, from floor to ceiling. Then Richard put in a wonderful light that turned on automatically when you opened the closet door.

When we were finished, Val showed me how to line up all the black pants and one black skirt, each on its own hanger, with all the hangers pointing in the same direction, and the same for all the white blouses. When I stepped back, there was enough space in between each hanger to see each piece of clothing!

I stood there, awed. This feeling went *beyond* ORDER.

I felt as if I had just stepped into a Zen meditation hall with its deep silence. "How do we lower our own noise?" Nancy has asked. Now I had one answer.

Every time I open the closet, I feel the abundance of how much I do have.

"Minimalism has nothing to do with lifestyle," said John Pawson, a well-known architect-designer of the style. "It has to do with feeling. If having nothing but a wooden stool in your living room makes you feel peaceful, you've achieved your objective."

Elegance is refusal. DIANA VREELAND, FORMER EDITOR OF *VOGUE*

While transforming the closet, I discovered an old trophy. I had forgotten all about it. Only when I held it in my hands and read the inscription, "Best Character," did I remember. Three years after my great sadness at not receiving this award at camp, I won it without even trying.

My disappointments I remember clearly. They are etched into my body and psyche. My victories are sometimes harder to recall. My intention is to give as much attention to my successes as I do to my disappointments.

Accepting success can also be a stretch.

A LOVE AFFAIR WITH CLAY

Art prepares the soul for tenderness.   ANTON CHEKHOV

I have had a love affair with clay for forty years.

It began when I was seven months pregnant with my first child, Michael. I stopped working as a teacher at New Rochelle High School, and, for the first time in what felt like forever, I wasn't programmed. I wasn't going to school, getting degrees, or teaching. I didn't have to be productive.

I was growing a child. That was enough.

I could play. I signed up for a beginners' class in pottery—making handmade objects—at Greenwich House in New York City. With no idea what I was looking for or what I wanted to do with clay, from the first moments I was smitten.

Adjectives like soft, tender, luscious, and human come to mind. Add to the list friendly, malleable, and resilient.

Clay is about *relationship*.

Clay is a wonderful teacher—it makes me pay attention. In making a piece, I am one element, but only one. My strong need to control has to take a backseat. Clay, if pushed beyond its limits, can become exhausted from overwork and start to sag, crack, or collapse—very much like us humans.

Am I working with or against the other element? If I am distracted, if I ignore what's happening right now with the clay (Does it need more water? Is it too moist?), the piece I have spent time working on may refuse to take part in our dance.

Clay, organic, living, changing, comes from the ground, and when I am working with clay, I feel grounded. The chatter in my head disappears and I feel ease—as if breathing fresh air.

I could have learned to make rectangles and square forms to match the furniture in our home, which is from a period of modern architecture known for its hard edge.

In contrast, I chose simple round forms—bowls and cups—and infinite small variations on these shapes, and I've been content for all these years working within that limitation.

Two elements coexist, the hard and the soft, the desire to control, to feel safe, and the desire to surrender to whatever is happening with the clay—or in my life. I want these two aspects to support each other, support me.

"Whenever we touch life, we shape it," M. C. said.

"We shape it with our warmth and caring, or with our coldness and haste, desire for power and money, desire for good rather than the GOOD. The power to heal and be healed is built into the body, into our clay body."

I would add: The power to heal and be healed is built into our bodies.

And a sensation in the body, once felt, begins to live.

TRYING TO CENTER

After Michael was born, I continued to go to Greenwich House, my one "extracurricular" activity in the week. During my second year, still enjoying making things by hand, the teacher asked, "Don't you want to *progress?* Don't you want to learn to throw a pot on the wheel?"

Finally, I did sign up for the class. And I did try to center a pot on a moving wheel.

But I never progressed.

Everyone else in the class was successful. To center a pot means to find a way to harness the moving energy of the lump of clay that has been placed in the center of the wheel, so you can begin shaping it into whatever you want. I couldn't do it.

Initially I was disappointed, but not devastated. Still, I felt the need to explain to myself why I hadn't progressed, so I came up with two theories.

THEORY ONE: Whatever object you're hoping to make, be it a bowl, cup, or cylinder, you have to be centered in order to find the center of the clay. I wasn't.

THEORY TWO: I didn't want to work with clay in a mechanical way. I noticed many of the eager students had as their goal to make a clay piece that looked perfect—machine-made. I wanted my work to feel and be handmade. I loved touching the clay at my own pace, without the spinning wheel.

Now, forty years later I'm ready to stretch—and see if I can throw a pot on the wheel.

It's never too late to be ready.

LIGHT

Blessed are the cracks—for they shall let the light in.

Someone handed me a scrap of paper with this quote after one of my talks, and I thought of Kevin, whom I first met seven years ago. The first time I saw a cracked pot he had made, I felt goose bumps. At his studio I saw more of his cracked pots—and saw beauty not only in all of them, but also in this forty-year-old man with a vision of helping children feel joy working with clay.

Months later Kevin showed me how to piece together my own cracked pot. When I held my pieced-together pot in my hands, I knew it would be an object I'd treasure—a symbol of self.

"It's not pots we are forming; it's ourselves," M. C. said.

Still standing there, taking in the power and beauty of this bowl, with all the same parts as before, but now totally different, I saw in every cell in my body:

To be whole doesn't mean we have to be perfect.

"You helped me plant a seed. You saw something in me."

Kevin said this as I walked into his brand-new ceramics studio.
I was about to take my first lesson in forty years on how to throw
a pot on the wheel. "If anyone can teach me to center clay on a
wheel," I told Kevin, "it's you."

"Centeredness is about change," he instructed.

"Centering is about movement. You can't get the clay centered
unless you get the wheelhead spinning and unless you move the
clay." He said he couldn't really tell me how to do it—the
language is in the body.

"It's kinesthetic," he said.

That's one of those words I've often heard, but have never really
understood. "Kinesthetic means it's in your body," he continued.
"You can't know with your mind how to center. You can't <u>try</u> to
be centered—you can't think, 'I should push here.' It just happens.

"You have to feel your way into it."

Something is *called forth* in me, I thought.

He didn't care if the clay wobbled a little at the beginning. "If it's not centered, it can still work," he said. "You can always center along the way."

I felt myself relax and grow *bigger than* when I realized I didn't have to have it all figured out in order to begin—just like my writing process.

"There's no right way to do it," Kevin said.

A glorious thought. When I heard that, I was ready to sign up for a lifetime in lessons.

How reassuring it is to remember that if we lose our way, we can find it again.

We don't have to be centered all at once.

We can center along the way.

As we become older, art and life become the same thing.
GEORGES BRAQUE

"Enough talk," Kevin said. "Let's get down to work!"

I turned on the switch to the electric wheel. Nothing happened. I tried a few more times. Kevin jiggled the switch and walked around testing various sockets.

"I lost my power," he finally said. "We blew something BIG!"

"Maybe I'm so powerful I've short-circuited it," I joked.

"Or is this what happens when we don't own our power?" I wondered to myself, thinking back to Nelson Mandela's wise words:

Our deepest fear is not that we are inadequate.
Our deepest fear is that we are powerful beyond measure.

"We blew something BIG!" Kevin repeated, smiling.

Finally, he brought in power from the house via a very long orange extension cord. Kneading the clay, getting the air bubbles out, I formed the clay into a ball the size of a grapefruit and plopped it as close to the center of the wheel as I could.

"Slowly," Kevin said, as I put my hands on the clay. "How you sit, how you place your hands on and off the clay, each movement— all affect the whole process."

"Everything makes a difference."

Of course I love to be reminded of the power of slow, but trying to focus with the wheel spinning, the clay wobbling, trying to *do it right,* I felt out of control—and scared. Would I have been tempted to give up without Kevin's reassuring presence?

Pressing my hands as hard as I could, moving from the outside inward, I did what I thought was right, but no matter how hard I worked, the clay seemed to get more and more off center.

"Feel your way into it," Kevin said.

"Not you struggling, pushing it this way or that way. *Relax* into the force going around. Can you notice what's happening?" Not holding my breath, actually relaxing a bit, I was amazed to hear, after about ten minutes, Kevin say, "It's almost centered."

This good news distracted me.

I lost my concentration, and in a few moments I knew the clay was again spinning out of control. "You have to be here," he repeated, "not just going through the motions physically.

"You have to be *present.*"

"You're not just centering the outside of the clay—you're centering all the way through."

He put his hands on top of mine, as Kaz had done showing me the movement in calligraphy, and gently directed the motion, perfectly comfortable helping me start to feel what it should feel like in my body.

"See if you can let go and let it center."

"Many people believe their *muscle* is centering clay.

But it's not—it's more about how you're focusing—aware of what that clay needs to do."

When the clay was centered enough, not perfect, I began opening the form, then pulling the sides up, feeling great sweetness in this rather difficult process.

To my amazement there on the wheel sat my first simple bowl.

Morning Star and I began meeting for a brief hello whenever she was in town. We'd talk about life, lessons, and stories that inspired us. I told her about getting goose bumps when four-year-old Kyle said, *"I'm bigger than that!"*

We had made a date to meet for tea, but when I heard she wasn't feeling well, I left her a message: "Take care—whatever that means."

"I'll take two cares and see you on Tuesday," she said.

I must have been particularly dense and also forgotten the message I had sent, so when we did meet I asked, "What did 'Take two cares and see you on Tuesday' mean?"

"In Portuguese it's called *tomando canto*—drinking care. Filling oneself up with special and gentle attention. It seemed to me," she added, "this is better than aspirin. And it worked. I feel wonderful today."

She believes drinking care is a way of making oneself bigger and better. "Self-criticism inspires shrinkage," she added. "We learn how to shrink—it is not part of us.

"To drink care is an expanding experience."

RELEASE

Nancy began the class by asking us to look at whatever was causing us discomfort—the neck, back, shoulder. Instead of labeling it as pain—could we see it as something *bigger than that*—a part of who we are right now?

"Your hip is calling for more breath," she said, looking at me.

"We all have a basic need for more breath in our bodies. She encouraged us to breathe into the part that was feeling sore or vulnerable—to make more space for our pain.

Lying there, I finally noticed how much energy it takes me to gear up to do so many things. I have too much practice trying to hold everything together.

"Could we *gear down?*" Nancy wondered.

"We rush so we can later relax. Instead, start relaxed."

"Dwell in what's soft," she continued. I liked the feel of that and closed my eyes and lay very still. "You don't have to work so hard anymore," I said to my hip, allowing it to relax into the floor.

When class was over, I didn't want to move. I thought I could lie there forever, soaking up a feeling of deep well-being. And my hip didn't hurt. By softening I was able to stretch and release some of the energy I was using to hold everything together.

"Could you find a release from your struggle?" I remember Mitzi once asking, "one that feels good and doesn't require so much hard work? A gentler way to change?"

Looking at the word *release,* I had seen *ease* tucked in.

Richard was in Japan, and my assignment was to look at his e-mail. Feeling intimidated, overburdened, and a bit resentful at being given a task I wasn't good at and struggling to "get it right," I saw a message on the screen.

Memory is tight. You may need to close some windows, move messages out of your IN, OUT, and TRASH mailboxes—or increase Eudora's memory size.

Then, I was given two choices:

LIVE DANGEROUSLY		QUIT

"I'm always going to be five-foot-two," a friend said. "Till I get to five-foot-one. "I will never reach the top shelf in my kitchen. Either I'll get a stepladder—or put nothing up there!"

"And I'll always be an earnest seeker," I said.

"That's part of my nature. I paused for what felt like a long time, and added, "I must have come from a long line of strugglers.

Maybe I will always struggle. But once I accept the part I can't control, stop struggling with struggle, I have choices. When I accept my limits, there's a wide range of possibilities I can tap into."

"Yes," she agreed. "You're working within God-given limits."

When we announced to our two sons, who were six and seven at the time, that we were going to leave New York City, where we lived in a very small apartment, and move to Berkeley, California, in the same breath we promised, "We'll have a house with stairs and a dog."

Almost immediately we got Boom Boom, a golden retriever we all grew to love. Years later, both sons went off to college, and Boom Boom, who was epileptic, stayed home. Eventually he got very ill and had to be taken to the hospital for a long stay. Back and forth he went from home to the hospital, not responding to the medicine. He was thirteen years old at the time.

Finally, the doctor suggested we *put him to sleep,* an odd expression, I think, as I write these familiar words. I didn't know what to do. I was tempted. He had had a full life—but I was also concerned about my *shadow* side—my motives—was I moved solely by compassion for Boom Boom?

Was expense a factor, the long hospital stay, and the discouraging prognosis? Even worse, was I too selfish to care for a very sick dog if he came home? I didn't know. I wanted to be the kind of person I'd like to think I am—so I stayed stuck.

We visited Boom Boom often, and I wondered what my sons would have wanted. Obviously, with all those murky questions in the air, I couldn't put him to sleep. Back and forth. Neither decision sat well.

When the vet called to say Boom Boom was unable to eat, drink, or take his medicine, I went to visit him. He lay there quite still.

"Boom Boom," I said, "you have to give me a sign. I can't decide on my own. I <u>need</u> you to tell me what your *spirit* needs."

I had never contemplated having a conversation like that with my dog, but at the time it seemed perfectly natural.

The next morning the vet called to say Boom Boom was better and we could come and take him home. We were given a very large container filled with cans of delicate dog food. He was still very weak, hardly able to get into the car.

At home, he just lay there in his favorite spot in the kitchen. He didn't eat. Or drink. Or take his medicine. When I asked if he wanted to go outside into the pen to watch the life on the street, one of his former delights, he just lay there, getting weaker and weaker.

As I watched him, the fog of indecision lifted.

He had made his choice. The decision was now easy. We called the vet to tell him we wanted Boom Boom put to sleep. "A good choice," he said.

As we drove to the doctor, Richard and I reminisced with Boom Boom about all the adventures we had all had with him. Though he just lay there, I like to believe he was listening. Never having seen an animal die, either naturally or by injection, I had horrid images of what his last moments would be like. The vet suggested we not wait for the actual injection, because there were many patients ahead of us and the wait would be long. We choose to stay.

When it was finally time for the injection, Boom Boom rested his head on my lap. No dreadful sounds or contortions followed. In less than a minute he was dead.

I could report to our sons what had happened with an open and peaceful heart.

Until then, nonattachment had been just a word. This was a *direct experience*. After a lot of holding on, not trusting, I was able to give up both my control and my need to come up with the *right* answer.

Since then, when I am particularly torn, I get out of the way of my judgments and go back to that question, either for myself or another.

What does my spirit need?

What does your spirit need?

"Boom Boom was a great spirit teacher," I told Laurie.

"My darling cat, Chloé, is 'at the end,' my vet says," she told me.
"So I am quite misty-eyed these days. I have to inject water into her
skin with a needle! This takes more courage than I thought I had."
She paused, then added,

"Courage driven purely by love."

Once a week, I walk with a friend at 5:45 A.M. This particular morning it was pouring. "You're crazy to want to walk in this downpour!" my walking partner said. For weeks, I'd seen the stationary bikes lined up in the hallway I have to pass through to get to my gentle stretching classes.

Motivated by a great desire to exercise before settling down to write, I decided to drive to the studio and join the 6:00 A.M. class. It's called "Cycling" or "Spin"—I'm never sure which.

I assured myself, "It's only a bike. Why not try?"

Eight people were already pedaling when I arrived. Not Amazons, but lean, like the bikers in their tight bright-colored outfits who zoom by us humans up the steep hills in my neighborhood.

Loud salsa music was playing. The teacher got off his bike to help me adjust my seat. "Turn the dial to the right to a five," was his first instruction. I found the black dial easily enough, but I kept squinting to find the marker for five. After fumbling unsuccessfully for a while, but wanting to *do it right,* I raised my hand. "I can't read the numbers."

"There are no numbers," he said. "It's all in your head."

It's all in my head? What in the world does he mean?

As I strained to follow his directions, I heard, "Get up on the bike."

The others raised themselves up off their seats and were standing and pedaling at a brisk rate. I couldn't even imagine the coordination or logistics it would take to perform that feat—another pivotal moment when I was tempted to bolt.

Was it morbid fascination, stubborn determination, or simply curiosity that kept me there?

At the next "up on the bike" I did try to mimic them, but quickly retreated to the relative comfort and safety of my seat. After a while I understood that farther turns to the right on the mysterious black dial meant the workout was getting harder. To the left, which we hadn't been instructed to do yet, would be easier. At eight, my wheels locked.

"Too much resistance," he said, but I was delighted to get this unexpected breather. It didn't last long because I was then told to turn my dial to the left until the pedals moved again.

Somewhere during class something in me surrendered.

I stopped trying to keep up or measure myself against anyone else in the class. *Against* isn't a very friendly word. Whatever I was able to do on the bike, even if I never got to feel comfortable standing up, I was totally focused and engaged in a first-class A-plus workout.

Surrender. A wonderful revelation.

"Imagine you're going up a really steep hill," the teacher said, during my second bike workout. Since I was huffing and puffing, this wasn't hard to imagine. Next, I heard him say, "Stay with me.

"Work through your resistance!"

Working through resistance is something I can understand. But a concept is different from actually working through resistance in my body. The freedom not to have to compare myself to the others opened a space for me to try standing up while peddling for a minute or two, before a wave of anxiety again brought me to my seat.

"What does 'Work through your resistance' mean?" I asked, when the class was over. "It's about your perceived level of exertion," David, the teacher, said. "Rate of perceived exertion, RPE, it's called. From zero to ten."

0 = sitting on a couch
10 = climbing Mount Everest

At zero, you're sitting on a couch. At five, you're still breathing normally and can carry on a conversation, but at ten, you are almost totally out of breath—climbing Mt. Everest. "You have to monitor yourself," he continued.

"Is there a system where you can compare yourself to someone else?" a woman had asked during the cycling. The teacher's answer was clear. "NO. That becomes competition.

"Your own heartbeat is your best guide.

"Group cycling is not competing against others," he added. The people who designed the machine deliberately took away the numbers.

An important lesson to remember: on a deeper level no one can tell me what is the right thing to do for myself. Something easy for my teacher, and for many in the class, will be difficult for me.

Two choices, speed and resistance. At times, the teacher asks us to go faster; at others, to move the black dial—which no longer seems so mysterious—to an eight, which is a hard push, going up an imaginary hill.

After a long uphill effort, our reward was a turn to the left and speed downhill. The heavy stable bike wasn't going anywhere. Still, fear whooshed up from memories of biking in Amagansett, Long Island, when I was scared going down a steep hill, and kept my foot solidly on the brake all the time.

I felt safer with uphill effort.

"Downhill tests your fearlessness," David said.

There's nothing wrong with pushing myself at times. But there's a fine line between doing the best you can, and overreaching—where you can make yourself sick.

"I trust my instinct about cycling," I told Nancy. "It's certainly an unfamiliar exertion, but it feels really good for my body—*and* spirit."

"It's a great idea," she agreed. "Cycling gets your energy moving—and it blows out the cobwebs."

She drew a big circle in the air around my head and said, "It takes the spin out of your thinking, takes all that energy that swirls around, and streamlines it to run it through your whole system.

"You're stretching into all the places you don't yet live in yourself."

I thought back to my black-and-white clothes. If I did only gentle exercises or only cycling, it would be limiting. For me, having more choices, more frequencies feels good. I don't have to be gifted at any of them in order to feel pleasure.

Now, I want to linger when class is over.

I splash cold water on my face and feel not only relief at having gotten through another class, but joy in welcoming this new experience into my body.

As I drive to Café Milano to begin writing at 7:15, I think of the woman on the StairMaster who had chosen Himalayan Trek as her program—when I had picked Walk in the Park.

"Nothing will daunt me the rest of the day," she had said. Refreshed, I now think,

"Nothing will daunt me the rest of the day."

GROWING WINGS

What brings about those surprising shifts that open our hearts and prompt our spirits to soar?

SQUARE ONE

"Ofer, I'm scared," I announced. I was discouraged in every cell. My hip, which had been hurting, had finally recovered after I went on a vacation with Richard and we walked for hours on level city streets. Five days after I came home, the pain was back.

Was it the vacation itself? Was it being away from my lists? Did my body simply prefer walking to sitting at the computer and writing in coffeehouses? "I can't just spend my life walking for hours," I told Ofer. "I have work to do. I feel like I'm back to square one."

"Well, you could look at it that way," he said, "but remember, you have gained knowledge of yourself. What you can do for yourself is greater than it was before.

"It's impossible to go back to square one."

One stretch in Nancy's class has stumped me for more than three years. Her instructions are clear: moving slowly, place a bolster parallel to the wall, then sit on the edge of it, lie back, and bring your legs up the wall, using your elbows to wiggle close.

Once in position, buckle your thighs together with a long strap, place an eye bag filled with flax seeds over your eyes—and relax. After a few tries, most people "get it."

Not me.

Each time I have to gear myself up to the task, glancing from left to right hoping to get a clue from my neighbor. Nancy usually sees me struggling and comes over—or I signal for help. Once I'm assembled correctly, this *antigravity* position is very relaxing.

This time as I struggled, Nancy whispered, "Maybe you've never given yourself enough time to puzzle out how to do this."

"*Take your time*—however long it takes to understand it—or not understand it!"

Goose bumps, my direction finder, appeared on my skin. She must have seen a lightbulb of recognition on my face, because she asked, "What happens inside as you try to do it? Does it remind you of anything?"

Absolutely. This time it's not a long-buried memory but a vivid experience. When I was five years old my mother, a great natural athlete, signed me up for a dance class. It was easy and fun moving my body to music—with no restrictions. I did so well that the following year the instructor suggested I go into an advanced class. My mother agreed.

I was now in a beginner's ballet class.

I have a lasting memory of seven young girls all going in one direction—and me heading in the other. I was trying especially hard, but, not knowing my left from my right, I had no way to understand what I was being asked to do. I couldn't do something I was expected to do. I felt overwhelmed and miserable.

I panicked.

That only made trying to figure out the teacher's instructions more difficult. In that moment, sixty-one years ago, I froze. I wanted desperately to fit in and I felt hopeless—a total failure. I refused to go back.

"You don't have to fit in, " Nancy said softly when I told her this story. "It's too high a price."

"There's a new day today—you don't have to wear yesterday around," Morning Star had said during one of our visits.

As I walked to my car after class I thought, "I've had a lifetime of yesterdays." Now I had another choice—and a clear intention. I'd find out when the studio was empty and take all the time I needed, see if I could slowly get my body to figure out her instructions.

A week after this conversation with Nancy, I went into the empty studio and with no one helping, instructing, or watching, put my feet up on the wall as if this particular problem had never existed.

A wise man is never in a hurry.   ARISTOTLE

"I've had three sessions with a body worker," M. C. announced, "and I found myself asking, 'What have I gotten from it? Let's get to it! Is anything happening?'" Then she paused, thought for a moment, and added, "Some things take time. Some things can only happen through time.

"They only happen—*time carries them.*"

Another wise friend, Joseph, told me, "For the next ten minutes, Sue, you have all the time in the world."

Near the end of a class with Ofer, during another of those exercises that are particularly challenging for me to understand, he gave an instruction I could follow without struggle or difficulty. Though we're not supposed to talk while the lesson is going on, I blurted out:

"I must be doing something wrong. It's so easy."

"That's a good one, Sue. You'd better write that down!"

When I was forty years old, I went back to graduate school. I can't remember much of what I learned in those years, but the first day, in the first class, the teacher told us,

"I travel through life with a light knapsack."

That image spoke to me then and has stayed with me all these years. To move through life with a light knapsack I have to order my priorities.

I can't **choose them all.**

I spend a lot of time before I travel sorting and paring down what I will take to absolute essentials. I'm pleased when I get on the plane for trips of up to three months with only two soft black bags, which I insist on carrying onto the plane myself. Recently, a friend handed me a scrap of paper with a quote:

Simplicity is making the journey of this life with just baggage enough.

Richard laughs at how much time I spend obsessing about what to choose. I do want to look "good" at certain times, and there are all those vitamins, art supplies, books, magazines, and the extras that accumulate at the last moment. I feel I'm being tested each time.

It's gotten a little easier with practice. And I'm committed to the end result—feeling uncluttered and delighted to be traveling with a light knapsack.

Sometimes we want something and its opposite at the same time.

Last June, feeling smug with my light luggage, I had to unexpectedly stay an extra two days in the town where I was giving a talk. A shop with wonderful black-and-white clothing was the devil's temptation. I'd been looking unsuccessfully for three years for something new to buy. I now faced a non-life-threatening decision—pulled between pride and desire.

"I can be flexible," I finally told myself. "My real challenge is to know when to be spartan and when to give in." In the end, I chose a pair of black pants, a black skirt, and a pair of shoes—almost doubling the size of my *virtuous* luggage.

I thought some more about my virtuous luggage. It's not just that I like being spartan. When I take less, I'm creating a space for possibilities.

Leaving stuff out allows me the possibility of putting stuff in.

WEEDS

While traveling, I wondered whether I might let go of another old and deeply ingrained habit—collecting thousands of scraps of paper filled with anything and everything that has reached out and touched me. Then I found this quote from Anthony de Mello:

A distraught gardener sent letter after letter to the Department of Agriculture, asking for advice. The last response read: "We have no more advice on how to rid your garden of weeds. We suggest, therefore, that you learn to love them."

Since my piles don't go away, can I learn to love my weeds?

I was reminded again of the *slender threads* that move us forward.

For years I've had an invitation to join a group in San Francisco that meets once a month at a friend's house. A teacher is invited and the format is always the same—a short meditation, usually for half an hour, followed by a talk, then a question-and-answer period.

Reluctant to be caught in rush-hour traffic and still afraid of driving in the dark, I've attended only a few times, always wishing I didn't set up limitations.

While I was staying at Alev's house, five minutes away from where the group meets, I had the luxury of walking over to the meeting. I was thrilled to have this chance to hear and sit with Ram Dass, the invited speaker, an inspiring teacher. By 3:30 he hadn't arrived, so our hostess suggested we begin the mediation without him. She asked someone else to lead us. If Ram Dass was able to come, he would just join in. We knew he was recovering from a severe stroke.

First reaction: disappointment.

Distracted, caught in my *wishing,* I did hear the instructor suggest we pay attention to our breath, especially exhaling. Meditation is something I know is good for me, but I have resisted it. And with my sore hip, even sitting was hard.

We gathered in a room with wonderful light, a quiet space in the midst of the city. No words, no motion. Feeling included as a part of the group, I noticed I could listen to my breath and begin to relax. My hip even quieted down. The silence grew deeper and deeper.

After fifteen minutes, there was a little rustle. I wondered if Ram Dass was now with us. It would be cheating to peek, but I did notice I was still attached to hoping it was him. Once in a while a man's voice said a few words—mostly about silence. Whose voice was it?

The silence in the room deepened.

In that silence, something shifted.

I began to appreciate that whoever it was, his words and the sense of being embraced by silence created a warm, golden glow that I could sense even with my eyes closed. My longing for what I thought I wanted—to have that voice be Ram Dass—disappeared.

I had never sat in such deep stillness. Did it matter who or what had created this atmosphere? We were all part of this creating.

A gong rang three times. The sitting was over. We could open our eyes and be present in the room. I didn't want to rush to see who was sitting in the chair. I savored being surprised. When I finally looked up, there was Ram Dass. He was in a wheelchair.

He now spoke much more slowly because of his stroke. He would also stop in the middle of a thought and pause. The pause didn't feel abrupt; he would raise his head a little to the left, be very still—and wait. Wait for words to come.

"The inner silence is I," he said. "The I of the soul."

"Silence is the method of getting to spirit."

"What happens in the silence?" someone asked.

"I search for the word—and the rest of the time I ski in the silence," he said, moving his left arm, his working arm, in a graceful movement, the way children pretend to fly a paper airplane.

"I was shocked when I heard you had a stroke," another person declared. "How could it happen to *you?*"

"I had the same reaction initially," he said. "Who is doing this to me? Do they know who ME is?! After the stroke I kept asking myself, 'Who am I?'" He paused.

"I was stroked."

"And that gave a demarcation to my life. Who was I then? Who am I now? This stroke happened to this body," he said, tugging at his green corduroy shirt. "It didn't happen to I."

With a twinkle in his eye, he told us that the doctor, the head of the hospital, came into his room and told him, "I've never had peace like I have in your room. How could you have a stroke and be peaceful?"

"You can use your instrument," Ram Dass told him. "You won't find me." Then he continued, "Things change, but I don't happen to be a thing. Nothing **I am** is changing.

"I used to play golf, loved to drive with a stick shift. I used to play the cello. Then I realized, This guy and that guy now—to compare them would cause suffering. If I was holding on to that, I would have said, 'I'm a person who used to play the cello.'

"I can make the stroke any metaphor I want. Do *you* know what it is?"

And then the longest pause of the afternoon. Each of us in that room was there with him in the pause.

"It's *hard grace*."

I didn't have a question to ask, but I did have a need to speak: "You talk much more slowly now than the last time I heard you," I said. "Now I feel your *presence* in every word. Your slower way, your pause, waiting for the next word to come, allows me to be *present*. Your *presence* has given each of us a present."

"When we try to say who we are, words can get in the way," he said. "Words don't explain that silence."

There was a break for tea, and I chose to stay near him, eager to hear more. A friend turned to me and whispered, "He's been pruned—like a tree."

"I'm so glad you agreed to give a half-hour talk," a man said. Ram Dass looked at him, "Yes. I will give a talk. I want to." "You don't have to talk for thirty minutes," I blurted out. "You can talk for five minutes. Or no words.

"Your *presence* will be enough. More than enough."

"Yes," he smiled, hugging my hand. **What I am.** Not words. Not what I have to say. That's the lesson I'm being a messenger for." He reached out again, grabbed my hand, and said,

"We <u>all</u> have heavy grace in our lives."

"Is there something I can pass on to others?" I asked, deeply touched. "I don't want anything," he said, and then looking at me with great tenderness, he added:

"Heart to heart resuscitation—you and me. All of us."

Lily Tomlin plays Trudy, a bag lady, in her performance of *The Search for Signs of Intelligent Life in the Universe*. Trudy has conversations with extraterrestrials. One night, Trudy and a few of her extraterrestrial friends went to a play. One of them tugged at her sleeve and whispered, "Trudy, look," pointing to his arm.

"Yeah, goose bumps," Trudy replies to the alien. "You definitely got goose bumps. Do you really like the play that much?"

"It wasn't the play that gave me goose bumps," whispered the extraterrestrial. "It was the audience." Trudy had forgotten to tell them to watch the play.

"I like to think of them out there in the dark, watching us," Trudy says to the audience. "Sometimes, we'll do something and they'll laugh. Sometimes we'll do something and they'll cry.

"And maybe, one day, we'll do something so magnificent, everyone in the universe will get goose bumps."

ALLOWING

Sometimes pure exhaustion opens the door for change.

I had just returned from giving a series of talks in the Midwest. Usually I come home bursting with energy, but this time I was deeply tired. A message blinked on my machine, an invitation to a workshop I had always wanted to join. It was given by two wise and sensitive leaders for a small group of women—all, I assumed, "interesting."

The sensible thing was to stay home and rest.

"But," I thought, "maybe there's something I can learn that would help." The day before the workshop, still feeling frazzled, I nevertheless made the effort to go into the city to get a haircut. This made no sense until I admitted to myself I wanted to look good. Not many people or situations trigger that old *hunger for acceptance* anymore, but the need is still in there, waiting to surface, and here it was, full-blown.

Twelve women who were indeed "interesting" gathered, and from the very first moment the leaders created a safe sense of community. We were asked to speak about ourselves for ten minutes sometime during the weekend. Normally that would not seem like a threatening request, but I had a strong visceral reaction:

I didn't want to open my mouth.

Usually I'm one of the first to speak up in a group. My *story* is in my cells. At the same time, I've been trying to get to know the three-year-old me, the child who learned to entertain her father—to perform, to do what I believed was expected of me, rather than what I wanted.

Even if this habit started as performance, after all these years wouldn't that now be me? I couldn't be sure.

What is performing? What is authentic?

The first night passed, and my hand didn't go up. The next morning at breakfast and then at lunch I remained quiet, listening, deeply moved by the honesty of each person's words, but still dreading my ten minutes. I didn't want to perform. Some deep, core part of me resisted. I wished, when my turn came, that I could say, "I pass."

I was the next to last person to speak. I can't remember exactly all that I said, but I began by describing what I was feeling in my body—that I had come to the gathering exhausted, and once I was there and stopped my usual moving around, I could feel the tired-ness under my being tired. That feeling scared me.

I spoke softly, not in my usual voice, which projects out there with much more forceful energy. I told of going for the haircut, wanting to look good, and wanting to make a good impression. It was a little like the time I had gone to a sweat lodge expecting a stimulat-ing experience and found myself terrified.

"I am very afraid," I had said out loud in the sweat lodge, in that same small voice. "I'm not sure I can do this. I may have to leave."

The circumstances certainly weren't as terrifying, but the voice had almost the same tone—open and vulnerable. I wasn't hiding who I was with *personality*.

No pretense. No trying.

I had always thought somewhere inside I wasn't big enough. And I would be disappointing to others if I didn't keep trying to measure up. But now I trusted enough to come from a place inside, tired, discouraged, unwilling to work hard trying to convince anyone I was anything but what I was at that moment.

My need to control, as best I could, an outcome had given way to *allowing*. I had tapped into a core strength. And when I finished speaking, the tiredness I had been feeling for almost a month dropped away.

I had become, without struggle, *bigger than that*.

I've never thought of trust as a *muscle*.

That weekend I felt I had stretched that muscle. I loved imagining myself going to the gym, working out—pumping iron—pumping my trust muscle.

I had glimpsed the courage to stop struggling.

A habit is just that—a habit.

Many of us, when we were young, developed strategies to survive and "fit in." We wanted to belong and did the best we could to belong. Now, we have embedded habits, behaviors and beliefs that no longer serve us.

Qualities learned can be unlearned.

Or when that isn't possible, we can <u>build better habits</u>. Then we have more choice. The next day of the retreat I had a chance to practice more choosing.

I did what I felt like doing.

I ignored my mind telling me what I <u>should</u> be doing. I didn't go to the yoga class, instead staying under the covers for that extra hour to read and be still—unheard of behavior from someone addicted to bolting out of the house at 5:30 each morning.

Later, we went on a long hike up steep terrain. I had believed that in order to protect my Achilles tendon, I shouldn't—couldn't—walk up steep hills. My foot didn't bother me, but when one of the leaders asked if anyone wanted to ride the rest of the way, I immediately said, "Yes." I didn't feel tired. I just didn't feel like walking anymore. That was reason enough. This may not sound groundbreaking, but for me this was risking new behavior.

The freedom to say "NO" was exhilarating.

The freedom to say "YES" to what I truly felt like doing was enormously freeing.

I felt I had no mask.

The second afternoon we were given rich, deep red clay, what I think of as Indian clay, and were asked to make whatever we wanted. Knowing from my books that I make ceramics, one of the women asked, "Aren't you going to have performance anxiety?"

"No," I answered. "I'm going to make a snowball."

That was indeed my intention. But after I made the snowball, I still had plenty of time, so I made a simple pinched pot—something I can do on automatic pilot.

The last morning we took a walk on beautiful land. We could pick up anything that spoke to us—flowers, fruits, pieces of discarded *whatever*.

I leisurely walked and talked with one of the women. I was in no hurry to pick things. Tempted, yes. But then when I thought more about a particular object or flower, it seemed even better not to have it. I enjoyed seeing the delight of many of the women amassing rich potpourris of things, and I was happy when some of the same things I had wondered about were selected by others.

The tiniest yellow flower, most likely a weed, finally caught my attention. The flower seemed to say, "Pick me."

Later we gathered around a large circle made of branches and flowers. Each woman put her collection in front of her and one by one we went around the circle and told what our objects meant to us.

When my turn came, I dropped the tiny yellow flower into the red colored bowl I had made without thinking about placement. I held the bowl in my hands and saw that my tiny flower had found just the right spot to land.

In every cell, I felt the simple beauty of the two.

The tiny yellow flower in the red bowl—the relationship they had with each other—these two objects were me. I saw their invisible vastness—ordinary and special, quiet and vulnerable, tender and strong and resilient.

I had shown the maskless person inside to the outside.

I could be vulnerable and safe.

AUDREY HEPBURN'S FEET

There is nothing original about adoring Audrey Hepburn.

Recently, I was surprised to read that she had big feet, a size ten. Ferragamo, the great Italian shoemaker, designed her shoes. "And she felt comfortable with herself," he reported.

"Why not heels?" someone asked. Apparently, wearing heels would have made Audrey's feet look smaller than the flats she always wore. Mr. Ferragamo answered,

"She didn't want to be anything other than the size she was."

M. C. was in the hospital, looking frail, her skin very white. Before going to see her, I called to ask if there was anything she would like me to bring. Her answer: "Café au lait, decaffeinated coffee, not espresso, with milk and a fat scone with raisins."

Before this unexpected stay in the hospital, she had planned to fly home to Pennsylvania; now she had a decision to make. She had given up her room—where would she go when she left the hospital? "It must be hard to plan your life right now," I said, speaking as someone who always makes lists and "plans."

"I don't do a thing," she said. "I don't go out and say, 'I must do something.' The messages I receive are in terms of physical feelings." She pulled herself up in the bed, just a little, enough to show she was an active participant in her life.

"Yes, I feel open to the quirks of fate. And I want to be."

One part of M. C. wished to remain in California, away from the cold winters in the East. "I can see myself fitting into the California hills," she smiled broadly, "as if I am *in* my life, not separated from it.

"I want to feel I'm in my life—not traveling around looking for it."

The next time I visited her in the hospital, I reported that I say her words slowly three times each morning as a wonderful reminder as I'm about to go out of my house:

I want to feel I'm in my life—not traveling around looking for it.

"I don't have to be doing much in my life in order to feel that," she continued, smiling. "I don't think it's introspection." "What is it?" I asked.

"I'm floating," she answered.

"Every once in a while I get a message—if I'm ready or not."

How wonderful it was to sit in a quiet hospital room with a beloved friend, still very weak, whose spirit was anything but weak. Holding her hand, sometimes passing her a bit more scone, and listening. Listening.

"Can you tell me more about floating?" I asked.

"Oh, yes," she replied, eager to say more. "I feel as if I were floating on a raft, not adrift but softly buoyant, supported in empty space by the wishes and prayers of my friends. I'm neither awake nor asleep—I'm in a cosmic doze.

"Like Polaroid film," she continued.

"Little by little I'm beginning to see some faint color, shapes, details, even the landscape out my window." She sat up a little and pointed, "It's like the clouds out there on a beautiful day," she said, looking out the window.

"Floating means something that supports us by mystery, and unknown forces."

Not wanting to wear her out, sensing it was time for me to leave, I bent down to kiss her, gave her the gentlest of hugs, and whispered in her ear, "I don't want to disturb you with any more talk. I think I'll go out and practice your kind of floating today."

In a now small voice, for she was indeed tired, she reminded me:

"There's so much to support you, Sue.
"Maybe you don't know that yet."

"Yes, M. C., we <u>all</u> need to trust that support."

"What are you doing these days," friends asked M. C. when she returned home to Pennsylvania.

"Nothing," she answered.

They didn't understand, and if they did, they were concerned for her. "It must be hard not to be working with clay," another friend said. "No. It's very easy," M. C. said. "Easy to be without these expectations.

"My creativity is busy and happy," she continued, "making a new relationship to my body. Indeed, making a new kind of person: slower, more conscious of walking, eating, and talking— unhurried, pleased with human tenderness and assistance.

"It's like living in another culture—released from old habits of *push* energy. I'm finding new ways—unaccelerated, unamplified, listening. Quiet. I like it."

The doctors told her she should rest ("As if I had any alternative!" she added), and she has enjoyed coming to know the mystery and secret joys of REST: "To sit in a corner on a rocking chair, being a presence in the house, not doing anything in particular."

"I don't have to justify my existence."

To celebrate this new creative way of being she sent me a poem she had written:

I PREFER TO BE IDLE

To be idle
To be in time
To have time
This I like best

LOVE'S STRETCHING LESSONS

How do you stretch your heart?

There were goose bumps when I read those words. They were in a note I found in my mailbox at the artists' colony. The night before, I had given a talk to the group on my work.

"You must have a big heart already to even ask such a wonderful question," I told Andy.

How do you stretch your heart?

Though I have been married for forty-three years, I am not an *expert* on love. I do feel excessively blessed. We are not a "death do us part" marriage, with all the stiff resolve that implies, but it is responsive enough to grow, not always gracefully, with each new challenge. I can tell you a little of my experience with *romantic love.*

I married Richard for many reasons. One of the clearest was I didn't want to turn out like my mother—a strong individual I admired in many ways, feared in others.

Even as a child, it was painful to hear how she spoke to my sweet, beloved father. She was the *bad* one; he was the *saint*. At some point in my growing up, I must have vowed unconsciously that I would <u>never, never</u> do that to a man—to any person.

Years later, I could see my parents with more realistic eyes, and I could feel how difficult it was for my mother to relate to my father. He was great at denying his feelings, digging in his heels, avoiding confrontation at any cost. I began to see their bickering as a dance and called it the *Mic and Mac Show*. They really did love each other.

My solution was to marry someone I would look up to.

I knew many men who were bright, certainly brighter than I was, but I still feared I might become critical like my mother. Richard was keenly intelligent, sensitive, kind, with a deep poetic nature. I placed him up there on a pedestal. With him, I would never turn into a shrew.

I also believed that Richard, a fine architect, would never succeed financially. He was too pure, not the type who would charm his clients, and I assumed that was what he needed to do to succeed. I would always look up to him, so if we were forever poor, it would be worth the price.

Richard was at graduate school in architecture when we first met, and one of his professors invited him to work in his office in Zurich, Switzerland. We married and sailed the same day to live there for two years.

Before we left, I provided for the future by filling a trunk, one of those old metal camp trunks, with long, to-the-floor "hostess robes." My father worked for his brother and they manufactured them. The trunk would be left at my parents' apartment until we returned from Europe. I planned to cut the robes off at the knee and use them as dresses.

"I'll never have to be a burden to Richard," I explained to myself. "He'll never have to buy me clothes."

I had been working as a teacher at New Rochelle High School just before we left for Europe, and my only excuse for such dependent thinking was that this was forty-three years ago and the world was different.

We found a room in a large house in Zurich, where we shared a bathroom with four other people and a kitchen where each of us had our own hot plate. I clung to the idealized image of the person I loved. Being poor remained a romantic choice.

We returned after two years to New York City. I went back to teaching at New Rochelle, and Richard taught at Cooper Union and Columbia. He also worked for a worldly Viennese architect who had talent and great charm.

When we decided to move to California, we sold our small co-op apartment in Greenwich Village, overlooking an air shaft in one direction and another modern building in the other, for more than the ten thousand dollars we had originally paid. This was all the money we had. In Berkeley, for the money we received for our co-op we were able to buy a big Spanish house in the Berkeley Hills.

A few years later, Richard became chairman of the Department of Architecture at the University of California at Berkeley and, later, Dean of the College of Environmental Design.

"How did he succeed?" I wondered. "Had I made a mistake? Did I fall in love with the wrong man?"

On one level, of course, I was happy and grateful not to be poor, but a part of me was confused by all this good fortune. For years, a part of me needed to tell anyone who walked into the house, "This isn't the *real* me. I've always lived in very small city apartment."

I had to adjust from the falsely ideal to the genuine and real.

Richard <u>was</u> who I always thought he was and *bigger than that.*

I asked Mitzi, who has been married for fifty years, if she had anything to add to love's stretching lessons. She paused, a long pause, and said:

"Love itself is on trial in a long marriage.

"With each physical loss, with each new dependence on the other, partners are tested to the limit. Can we love when we are so different physically from the time we fell in love? Can we survive X-ray intimacy?

"Intimacy exposes our defects, the habits we don't like, the infuriating differences in opinion. We must stretch to accept our partner's limitations, put them into the larger context of the person's whole being, family history, genetic endowment—see their essential 'humanness.'

"And then maybe our loved ones can forgive us for not being perfect, either."

With each test of love, Mitzi actually finds her love expanding. "I have discovered that the essence, the core of love, is so much deeper than the heady attraction of early love. When we see compassionate love reflected in each other's eyes, when we laugh heartily at the same jokes, when we hold hands as we walk, I feel something far beyond happiness. I feel blessed."

When a long-term partnership works, she believes a mysterious transformation occurs, something she could not have anticipated in her early years. "Our home has become a magic haven," she continued, "a safety zone, and our 'enchanted cottage.'"

I had seen and remembered the old movie *Enchanted Cottage*. The hero is a plain-looking man and the heroine, a homely woman.

"They fall in love, marry, and buy a simple cottage to live in," Mitzi remembered, "and whenever they enter their home, each is immediately transformed into the ideal romantic partner, beautiful inside and out. The camera shows how they each looked to the outer world, and then how magnificent, how special they looked in each other's eyes. They become glamorous to each other. Love is the miracle that creates their enchanted cottage."

"I think you're right," I told Mitzi. "In real life we often do not see each others as our mirrors see us."

Mitzi, who is eighty, shifted to talking about herself and her relationship now. "Though we recognize the limits of our lives and see the end approaching, here, in our home, we are not just two old people. We are all the ages and all the different selves we have ever been.

"As you would say, Sue, through these stretching lessons of the heart, I have achieved *hard grace*.

"My heart is full. It is not heavy."

It was obvious to all who knew M. C., and certainly to M. C., that her robust energy was waning. For a while she took up knitting and knitted, as she did everything she took on, with great enthusiasm and gusto.

She was quite proud of a handsome scarf, multicolored, that looked like one of her vibrant paintings. She had just made it for a friend, and when she announced that she would like to knit me a scarf, I was thrilled.

"I'm a bit concerned about the color," she smiled, knowing my limited color palette. I told her what she already knew. I like white. I like black. And maybe a bit of gray. We laughed about the various mutations in my color range, until I finally said, "I would really love a white scarf."

My white scarf arrived a few weeks later, with a note in her distinctive handwriting:

Here is the while scarf I have knitted for you.
There are a few holes I didn't intend—pure poetry.
My knitting mentor says they are invented stitches.
Oh, well.

Holes for the soul to travel in and out.

I wear my white scarf proudly on all kinds of occasions even when I have no rational need for a scarf, but have a need to feel M. C.'s spirit embodied in the stitches.

M. C.'s wisdom wrapped around my body replaces my habit of struggle, and the scarf, with its holes for the soul to travel in and out, has become another new talisman.

UNEXPECTED

Leave room for the unexpected.

After *Plain and Simple* was published, I did what many writers do—gave talks at local bookstores. Before my first talk I was so nervous and flooded with feelings that I wondered if I could say a word. My son David, who sat with Richard in the very last row, seeing how emotional I was, told Richard, "If she starts to cry— I'm getting out of here."

The talk went well, and Richard grinned, "You're a missionary."

Meant as a compliment, his words made me uncomfortable. Then the telephone started ringing, infrequently at first, with invitations to talk. The groups extending the invitations became more and more varied: age, sex, geography, economic, religious, and political affiliations.

I spoke to womens' groups; at colleges and hospitals; an artists' retreat in New Harmony, Indiana; a wide spectrum of religious groups—Mormon, Presbyterian, Jewish, Episcopalian, Quaker, Buddhist, Friends Society, Brethren women ministers. I spoke at John Ascuaga's Nugget in Reno to the benefactors of a large medical center. And a women's conference in Vermont called:

WOMEN WITH WINGS

I had never suspected that I could stand up in front of a large audience and speak from my heart. And I was touched that a journey that had grown out of my own genuine struggles could be of use to others.

After a few years of giving these talks, I understood that Richard was right. I was spreading *spirit seedlings,* and I did have a missionary's zeal to share with others what I had learned— to raise the questions this journey had raised for me:

"What really matters?
Is there another way to lead a good life?"

I report this list not as an achievement but for a far more important reason. If I had not been thrust into this unexpected activity, I would have still believed my message was geared to a narrow range of people like myself.

The experience of meeting so many different people stretched my heart. I saw that underneath our real differences, many of us are more alike than I ever would have imagined. We share the same quest—to be our best selves—and make a difference to others.

After a meeting with an Episcopalian group in Arizona, the bishop stood up to thank me. He gave me a small pin, which I now treasure. It says:

We Are One.

"We're honoring six women in the community," the director told me, just before my talk in Salt Lake City. "Each of them has made an outstanding contribution. But it would be wonderful if you could tell each one of the nine hundred people in the audience:

'EVERYONE IS WORTH HONORING.'"

TRUST

"What is it we trust when we struggle?" Rachel asked one day, as we sat and had tea. I had asked her thoughts about the heartbeat of struggle. "I suspect it is ourselves alone," she said.

"What is it we trust when we find ease?"

"I suspect is something beyond ourselves," she continued, "whether in other people or in the greater universe. Perhaps this shift in trust is how the whole thing happens."

When our family came to California, I didn't know how to drive. Living in New York City all my life, I hadn't really needed to. For three years, I continued to live as though I were in New York City.

The fourth year, I learned to drive, but I only drove in Berkeley. When I went to San Francisco, I took the bus. Years later, one of my sons started college in San Diego, five hundred miles away, and, although he didn't say it, I sensed he was having a difficult adjustment. Of course, I could have taken a plane, but the truth was I wanted to see if I could drive to San Diego by myself.

There was no room for failure in this model.

I visualized all the possibilities.

If I drove for an hour, I told myself, and that proved to be as much as I could handle, that would be fine. And if I was able to drive two hours or three and then needed to turn back, that would also be fine. And if I went for a few hours and needed to stop and wasn't yet ready to turn back, I could stay over at an inexpensive hotel. And if it took three nights of staying over, that too would be fine. If I got to the edge of Los Angeles and felt overwhelmed by the maze of freeways facing me, I might turn back.

I gave myself permission to do what I could do—whatever it was—and accept that as success.

No judgment. No blame.

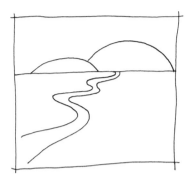

On and on I drove, enjoying a reassuring conversation with myself, carried along by a feeling of deep appreciation for my willingness to take on the challenge.

Starting out at 6:00 A.M., with many stops along the way, I arrived at the edge of Los Angeles at about two in the afternoon—between rush hours. Braving the maze of Los Angeles freeways, some of the hardest driving in the world, I kept going.

I had given myself so much permission, so much space to accept and appreciate whatever would happen that, nine hours later, I knocked at my son's door, and he looked at me, amazed.

Total acceptance of any outcome was a new way for me to meet a challenge.

What makes us wise one moment, and so unwise at another?

I still don't think of myself as a particularly good driver, but every once in a while, I love to drive down to Los Angeles by myself on Route 5. It's become a ritual. A celebration and recognition:

What I had learned in traveling was so much more than arriving.

SOUL WORK

"What are we going to birth this year?" a friend asked M. C.

"I'm birthing my death," she answers.

"Far from being intimidated," she tells me, "I feel an excitement, participation—something new." Then she continues, "I was surprised that I have the same interest as before—this is just the next thing.

"Something is going on in the creative process—if we let the fires burn and don't try to understand why everything happens." Then she adds, "I may not last much longer," stating this as a fact, not as a judgment. "I don't have a strategy, except a hope, as Yeats says, to 'cease upon the midnight with no pain.'"

"Backpacking the hereafter."

ANATOMY LESSON

In December, my friend's dog, almost too excited to see me, jumped up with such force that he pushed me down a flight of wooden stairs that led to their house. I've had something out of place in my left shoulder ever since.

Infraspinatous tendinitis the doctor called it and sent me to a physical therapist.

After watching me move my shoulder in various positions, Arlene, the therapist announced:

"Your wing isn't operating properly."

When I repeated this to Tamera, a friend and movement therapist, she said, "Your image of your wing and *the soul growing wings* needs to be made more physical. I think of my wings as the scapula, those two triangular bones that form the shoulder girdle. These angel wings literally slide across the spine, opening the chest." Gently I extended my arms, opening my chest and taking a deep breath.

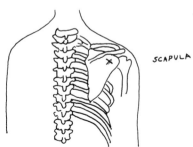

SCAPULA

I had spent a lifetime flapping.

Now I imagined myself an eagle, gliding high enough in the sky to take in the bigger picture—<u>and</u> the important details.

My old pattern of constantly flapping, struggling to stay in motion, had exhausted me, kept me off center, and made me feel *smaller than.*

At my next appointment, the therapist said, "Your wing still isn't stable. You need stability in order to have mobility.

Now I am aware and delighted when I do feel grounded—feel the ground. There's a weight to me then that has nothing to do with how much I actually weigh. And I notice I'm more light on my feet at those times.

Many years ago I volunteered to help a twelve-year-old boy who was run over by a car regain his ability to move. *Repatterning* it was called, an almost round-the-clock ritual, as friends, four of us at a time, would work with him, each taking an arm or a leg, moving it gently, hoping he would eventually re-remember how to use that part of himself.

One day in Nancy's class, I thought of that boy as she was saying that growth didn't have to come from pain, struggle, or other negative motivators. "Find a support that is not fear based. We could learn to grow through happiness."

"I'm being *repatterned*," I grinned, and my heart opened wide.

"Are you strong enough to stand happiness?" she asked.

"*Yes!*"

Donna, who had told me about the *space between* two concrete walls, filled with flowers, wrote to say she'd be coming to San Francisco for a visit. When we met over coffee, she was curious about my work. I always have trouble describing what I am writing about, but I mentioned stretching and "I'm *bigger than that*." "I have something that might fit," she said.

"When I was seventeen years old, just before my senior year in high school, a dreadful thing happened. I was sitting on the edge of my bed facing the mirror, rolling my hair in those awful pink curlers. My sister was in the bed next to me. Suddenly I felt a deep, sharp stab in my chest. I tried to take in a breath and was filled with overwhelming pain and a feeling of suffocation."

Fear gripped every part of her body.

She struggled to get air, able to take in only the tiniest of breaths. Her sister ran for help.

They rushed her to the hospital. An X ray revealed a weak spot on the lung that had bubbled and burst. The entire top of her right lung had collapsed. She needed major surgery.

"I was left with a very long scar that ran from just under my right breast," she said, pointing to where the scar began, "and then around my side, following up my shoulder blade and ending at my upper back.

"It was hideous.

"The scar reminded me of the horrifying days spent in that hospital, where I was drugged, poked, prodded, and punctured." Incredibly frightened and frail, Donna faced death and then felt as if she had been awakened from a sleep. "I began to question everything in my life. Who am I and what is life for?"

She learned to walk again on wobbly legs and returned to high school. After a year, she was fully recovered. Seven years later her other lung collapsed. Surgery was scheduled right away.

"Now I had another scar," she declared, "just as long and grotesque, on the other side of my body, a mirror image of the first one. These scars were hideous, gaping holes; the only good thing was I couldn't see the part of the scar that was on my back."

When she felt better, she was determined to change her life.

"I gathered up my shattered self, bought a very old, cheap car, left the Midwest, and drove to California. I loved the sun, the sea, and the freedom. "The beaches were bliss," she said, "but bathing suits were a problem. I was always self-conscious, unable to find a suit that could hide my scars and the horrible memories."

On a typical sunny southern California day, she and her close friend Linda headed to the beach. "Linda was listening to me moan in despair. I can still see her tilting her head slightly to the side," Donna recalled, "thoughtfully nibbling on the nail of her index finger as she looked at me and said, 'Donna, I don't think those scars look so bad.

'They look like the place where your angel wings were attached.

'They're just there to remind you that you really are an angel and once had real wings.'

"Linda's words were a gift of pure love that profoundly changed my life," Donna recalled with much tenderness. "Since then, I've never looked upon those scars in the same way, though it has taken many years to discover the truth in her observation."

Now when Donna sees her scars she remembers her wings.

"I feel their power and breathe life into them as if they are still really there."

Goose bumps.

With a great deal of feeling, she added, "Softly they unfold. My focus changes. My heart expands and I see through love as my friend Linda did.

"With these eyes I can see that each and every one of us has a pair of beautiful angel wings."

It was easy to imagine Donna's soul growing wings.

"I can feel my own wings beginning to grow," I told Donna, deeply moved.

Surprises are there for us—our stretch is to make room for them.

Though I continued to be intensely involved in writing, I still <u>never</u> thought of myself as a writer. "Oh, writing must come so easily to you," people would say, after I have given a talk or a reading. I am sure they meant it as a compliment, but each time I felt compelled to tell them a long story—reassuring them that writing was still the most difficult and unnatural task I could have ever imagined taking on, a true test. Then I would say to myself, "There must be a better way of doing this."

When writers asked about my writing process, I would state, "I'm not a writer—what I am doing is 'something else.'" I stumbled trying to explain what that "something" might be, and I'm sure many of them doubted the sincerity of my protestations. But I was sincere. Totally.

Over the last two years, I've made a certain kind of progress. When someone said something positive about my writing, I would pause—that famous lesson I am learning—take a deep breath, and say, "Thank you." Period. No story. I would smile, thinking:

"This is my *spirit* practice."

I thought I hated writing.
Why in the world I was doing it?

How I wrote did not in any way fit the picture I had in my head of how a writer writes.

Most writers I know save and savor their journals. I delight in tearing the pages out and throwing them away—saving some of the scraps to add to my ever growing piles of paper.

I wasn't totally naïve. I knew that writers have many different styles of writing, but I believed they all wrote sentences, no matter how many times they had to go back and rewrite them.

That's not what I do.

I've already said, I collect thousands of tiny pieces of paper, scraps, filled with words, ideas, quotes, musings—anything that reaches out and grabs at my heart. I trust there must be a reason for wanting and needing them—even if I don't know at the time what that reason is.

Dazzled and eventually overwhelmed by all these choices, I resist taking the next step: Choosing some of the fragments and putting them on eight-by-ten piece of paper with removable tape. The *removable* is essential.

I still want to choose them all.

Mitzi says she gets an Excedrin headache trying to imagine what it's like carrying all those little pieces of paper in my head. The piles keep growing and I keep moving them around, reordering, rethinking. Sometimes, I get so discouraged, I collapse.

Then I return to the task. I almost have to force myself to take some of the scraps and make them into a tentative sentence. After quite a while, a rough paragraph is formed. Relief comes when I begin editing and reediting, a great many times.

Finally, I see a simple sentence before me. I am amazed that it could emerge from this labor-intensive, out-of-control process. Magic, doubt, and a great deal of struggle are built into almost every sentence.

I never stop long enough to ask, "Is it worth it? Does it matter enough?" Once, thinking about a solution to that question, wondering how to proceed, hoping to keep fear and doubt off the front burner, and working on a new powerful computer that works faster than I can think, my fingers typed the word *solution*. I stared at it. Printed on the page I saw:

*Soul*utions

Six months ago, I was at the artists' colony, working as I always do—the way I have just described. When it was my turn to give a talk to the group about my "work," I decided, at the last minute, to invite everyone into my room to see for themselves *how* I work.

There was almost no empty space on the floor. No wonder I crave empty space in my closets and order and calm in my exterior surroundings! Every inch was covered with *possibilities.*

I no longer need to pretend, to spare myself or anyone else, to *seem* different than I am, so I told the group of my doubts, how in the five years it took me to write my first book, every single day I had to live with my rational mind saying:

"**STOP THIS!** You are wasting your time. You should be out there doing something useful." But a quiet, less definite voice said:

"Doubt if you must, but persist."

This back-and-forth dance of doubt and trust has taught me a great deal about faith, faith with a small *f.* Many of us have our own version of this challenging dance. It is important to remember:

It's the persisting that matters!

The morning after my talk, I began my routine as usual. I sat at the computer transcribing some of the pieces of paper that had been on the floor. Suddenly I said, and, more important, felt:

"I <u>am</u> a writer."

The simple clarity of that statement amazed me.

I felt goose bumps. They had indeed been a direction finder—the *goose bumps theory of intuition* made even more sense now than I had previously understood.

I saw that *how* I write is not the right way or the wrong way—it is just one way of writing. But it is <u>my</u> way. This was a revelation— and I felt it in every cell in my body.

Because knowing and owning this truth had taken so long, this awakening was even sweeter. "It's been a stretch," I said to myself, grinning.

When this journey first began and I looked at Pamela and said, "You are an artist," her face was shining. In that moment, before my mind had had a chance to catch up, I had seen a deeper-rooted truth, a truth *beyond* my usual knowing—

Each of us has our own way of expressing ourselves.
Each of us has something special to give.

And it is important to value our own way of expressing ourselves—
whatever it is.

Now, I repeat, as if it were a mantra:

Don't limit your vision.
Don't get attached to a specific outcome.

Something important may be right in front of you—but it may
come in a form you aren't expecting.

One day as I sat in Café Milano surrounded by my scraps, totally
immersed in what I was doing, an elderly woman came up to me.
She said, in a French accent,

"I've enjoyed watching you—the way you cut up the pieces, and
save what is important. What are you doing? You seem to be
having so much fun." She paused, and added, *"You should write a
book!"* I took her hand, held it, and said,

"That's what I am doing. I'm writing a book."

The possibility of sprouting wings delights me.

Sometimes, when I think I'll never be able to hold on to this new language of listening to my body, I think of the image of *our souls growing wings.*

"Wings grow out of your heart," Nancy said.

I was startled. She was talking about the real body. "Your arms and hands are an extension of your heart," she explained. "For your wings to be healthy and sturdy, the back of your heart has to open."

Mystery.

There's a backdoor, she continued, and placed her hand, as light and soft as a whisper, directly in the middle of my back. "Can you open the shutters?" she asked.

"Shutters?"

First a backdoor, and now shutters.

"What do you mean by shutters?" I asked. "Just like the shutters you put on your windows," she explained, "an extra board that covers up the window—an extra layer of protection from winter. Open them up!

"Let life in."

When I started this journey, I was yearning to let go of my habit of struggle. I hungered for ease. Kyle's words *"I'm bigger than that"* and Pamela's deeply felt "I'm not an artist" set off goose bumps— a wake-up call in my body.

And the goose bumps led to the image of *our souls growing wings.*

I have kept that image close to my heart. Could I stretch—grow wings—so my spirit could soar?

Wings seem to suggest that I want to fly, which I <u>do</u> want. But I was never interested in being a disembodied spirit—living only in the clouds.

My soul also wants feet, **big** sturdy feet.

"I want them planted firmly on the ground, grounding me," I told M. C. The image reminded her of an avocado pit sprouting. When the pit splits, a nub pops out and splits again. The sprout goes up toward the sky at the same time as the root goes down.

She's right. The avocado seed mirrors my impulse to rise up and also to go deeper—certainly a fuller, more robust sense of a life unfolding than I had imagined before I first felt goose bumps.

What I want is a soul with wings <u>and</u> big feet.

My wings may not be ready to soar, but I'm *"taking root to fly."*

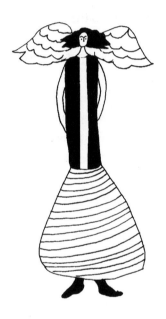

When I write I use the "I" voice—but I am always thinking **"we."**

We have been on this journey together. *Stretching Lessons* is about coming home to a deeper place inside ourselves. It is about opening our hearts and growing the wings of our souls.

And there will always be more to learn. There will always be mystery.

I still treasure the card a friend sent for Valentine's Day many years ago with the words of Rilke, written in her beautiful handwriting:

Be patient
toward all that is unsolved in your heart.

There is no shame in happiness.

ALBERT CAMUS

ACKNOWLEDGMENTS

Faced with the task of acknowledging all those who have stretched my heart, I want to say:

I CHOOSE THEM ALL.

Mitzi McClosky, my dearest friend, is an inspiration.

Laurie Snowden's graceful, intelligent editing made a huge contribution.

Val Lagueux's aesthetic of beauty and design make my heart sing.

Nancy Minges, teacher, guide and friend taught me about spirit through listening to whispers of my body.

Rachel Naomi Remen's profound wisdom was a rare gift.

Sandy Dijkstra is a remarkable agent and friend—fierce, wise and tender.

Liz Perle, my editor, is intelligent, imaginative, with a BIG heart and enormous capacity to inspire.

Jon Beckmann shared his deep wisdom and love of books with me.
Laurie Fox has sparkling creativity as a writer and friend.
Mary Ann Rafferty's vision and grace fill me with awe.

Pamela Atkinson and Kyle started me on this journey.

Loie Rosenkrantz, Donna Hepburn, Leah Stein, Mary Bisbee-Beek, John Parman, Kitsi Watterson, Kathy Dorhmann, and Sandra Sharpe are poets of the soul. Loren Liebenthal is a singular talent, brilliant and funny. Barbara Gates contributed rich insights Erica Deutsch has fresh mind. And Joanna Rose is simply amazing.

Lee Gruzen is a gifted writer and extraordinary friend.

Carol Ferraro is a beloved magician of spirit.

Jill and John Walsh, Ruth and Alan Stein, Joanna and Dan Rose, Joyce and Bob Menschel, Milt and Rosemary Okun, Peter Steiger and Esther Schoellkoff—are always in my heart.

Ofer Erez shared his powerful intelligence and clarity. Morning Star lives magic. Yvonne Rand, will always be my wise teacher. Ram Dass is a unique guide. Kaz Tanahachi's calligraphy and deep sense of purpose light a path for me.

"If you thank so many people," a friend said, "others will wonder if you wrote this book." I did write this book—and many wonderful people helped. Theo Gund, Anne Kalik, Diana Goldstein, Dru Gensler, Dorothy Buckley, M. J. Ryan, John Eberhard, Alev Lyle Croutier, Amy McCurdy, Patti Breitmann, Thaisa Frank, Catherine Lyon, Carol Field, Naomi Epel, Kay Montgomery, Betsy Scheiner, Suzanne Tiberghien gave wise guidance.

Jon and Barbara Beckmann shared their beautiful sanctuary.

Karina Epperlein, Joy Mc Comb, Gene Farb, Pat Millington, Ivy Ross, and Lorraine Weiss are powerful wizards. Tamera Greenberg, Gay Lee Gulbrandson, Paige Wheeler, Kathe Rothacher, Janet Welsh, David Parker, Deborah Stone, Diana Kehlmann, Betsy Kagin, Arlene Suda, Judith Langis, Dub Leigh, and Audrey Nakamura taught me body wisdom.

Kevin Nierman is awesome. Phil and Joanna Enquist, Nancy Selvin, Gale Antokal, Pat Hoffman, Sylvia Stulz, Sandy Simon, Bob Brady, and Jim Rosen are wonderful artists and friends. A special bow to Robin Chiang for being Robin.

I felt immense support from HarperSanFrancisco. Along with Liz Perle, THANK YOU to David Hennessy, Rebecca Fox, Eric Brandt, Terri Leonard, Margery Buchanan and Steve Hanselman.

Kendra Peterson and Harriet Blanton my "honorary" daughters, Chris and Fred Ford, Lon Addison, Judy Beck Durham, Angie Theriot, Natalie Goldberg, Ann Corcos, Annie Childs, Arlene Bernstein Jackie Wagner, Junko Shisedo Cook, Ellie Coppola, Barbara Bladen, Tomoe Katagiri, Katherine Koelsch Kriken, Harriet and Mort Cohen, Cecille Moochnek, Herb McClosky, Yvette Lehman, Morley Clark, Edith Kasin, Judith Shaw, Marilyn Levine, Martin and Maria Perez, Maritza Duarte, Saeng Sithandon, Dr. Ron Lee, Arthur and Helene Rosenfeld, Claire Held and Martha Halperin are valued friends and family.

The Djerassi Foundation gave me the gift of time. Blessings.

And to M. C. Richards, who died before this book was published, I offer my eternal love.

Gordon and Suzanne Chun are the remarkable designers of all three of my books. Their art made an immense contribution.

My love and admiration for my sons, Michael and David, continues to grow. Both of you, so different, share a deeper core— thoughtful, compassionate and strong individuals.

In the acknowledgment of *Everyday Sacred,* I called Richard a saint. Is there a category even bigger than that? Your artist/poet sensibility and love and encouragement light up these pages. Our "teamness" lights my life.